The Lord is My Agent, and He Only Takes Ten Percent

A Top Model Agent and Casting Director's

Journey of Faith in the High-Stakes

World of Fashion

TYRON BARRINGTON

ISBN 10: 0615973116
ISBN 13: 9780615973111

Table of Contents

Author's Note:

The names of most of the fashion industry people referred to in this story have been changed in order to protect their privacy.

Introduction

GOODBYE, DRAMA

"Then Moses said to the Israelites, 'see the Lord has chosen Bezalel, son of Uri, the son of Hur, of the tribe of Judah, and he has filled him with the Spirit of God, with skill, ability and knowledge in all kinds of crafts – to make artistic designs for work in gold, silver and bronze, to cut and set stones, to work in wood and to engage in all kinds of artistic craftsmanship. And he has given both him and Oholiab, son of Ahisamach, of the tribe Dan, the ability to teach others. He has filled them with skill to do all kinds of work as craftsmen, designers, embroiderers in blue, purple and scarlet yarn and fine linen, and weavers – all of them master craftsmen and designers." (Exodus 5 vs. 30-35)

It was February 2003. With my back turned to the agency where I once made my *Vogue* dreams come true, I closed my eyes, took a deep breath and smiled a Cheshire cat smile as I shook the dust off my feet on the welcome mat of the last agency for which I hoped I would ever work.

No more models.

No more castings.

No more bookings, confirmations and cancellations.

No more overpaid, selfish, insecure models.

No more greedy agency bosses for whom no amount of money was ever enough.

I let out a big sigh, cackled a bit and walked down the stairs to the street. I felt great. *This is how it feels to be free*, I thought. I felt like a prisoner whose sentence was up. I was cut loose from years of being trapped in a business I had once loved but now despised. No more being chained to a booking table doing hard labor, which for me meant guarding 'my models' from other agents while listening to them bitch, whine and complain about things pertaining to their oversized, insecure egos. Those included not being asked to shoot *Vogue* this month, someone getting more money than they did, not wanting to work on a given day because their boyfriends said something thoughtless or cruel, and putting on even a fraction of a pound. I was sick of fighting for bookings and constantly pimping myself to find work for spoiled women who never showed the slightest appreciation.

My days of flesh peddling were over. Freedom!

"No more drama!" Mary J. Blige's hit song resonates in my head.

"Thank you, Lord, and thank you, Mary J. Blige. You could not have sung it any better," I whispered to myself.

Tomorrow, I would be on a plane heading to the land of samba, Brazil. I would be at Carnival! Just the thought of being on a beach in Rio de Janeiro made me smile even more broadly. What better way to end a chapter in one's life and to start a new one? I could hear the beat of the samba drums and feel the heat and warmth of the Brazilian sunshine. I could feel the flip-flops on my feet and taste the iced cold coconut water. *Lord, I pray there will be gospel samba music in Heaven when I get there so I can dance before you like David did.*

I was walking out the door to a new life, not knowing exactly what I was going to do next but knowing that I was not going to be working for any modeling agency. For now, that was enough. I would no longer be attached by an umbilical cord to the dysfunctional world of high fashion, where the world would collapse if a model failed to show up for her assignment. I was going to catch up with the clouds and let them lead me wherever they would. I would no longer be a six-figure salaried baby sitter to infants with eating disorders.

AMEN!

The Ex-Boss

The drama of the fashion business had been an unwanted part of my life for years—all the way back to the tiny New York agency I had opened with my partner, Andrew, in 1989. It was the first day we opened our doors, and I had booked the first job for one of the three models I was representing. This was cool. I was excited and in a joyful mood. No, it wasn't *Vogue*, but, yes, we had our first confirmed job. Then came the call. I knew it would come, but I didn't expect it on the first day.

The phone rang. The voice said, "I thought you weren't going to work for another agency?"

A lump formed in my throat. It was my ex-boss, Bill. I had resigned from his agency a few weeks earlier, just before Christmas. Andrew and I had formed our own little boutique agency not too far away, but not too close. When I'd resigned, my boss asked me if I was going to work for someone else. I'd replied, "No." I wasn't. I wasn't going to work for someone else, unless you count the Lord as your boss. I was going to work for myself.

Forget the lump in my throat. Now I worried that I would wet myself. I calmly responded, "I'm not working for another agency. I'm working for myself."

That did not go over well. The flood of profanity came first, followed by the threats. "First, I'm going to break your knee cap then every other bone in your body. You're messing with the wrong person," my ex-boss said in a relaxed tone that made it sound as though he was sitting at a sidewalk café on a spring morning and ordering a cup of cappuccino.

I knew these weren't idle threats. That was terrifying.

My first thought was that I needed to get on a plane immediately and get as far away as possible.

During the time that I worked with Bill, other agents warned me to be careful around him. He was a man of few words, but he didn't need words to be intimidating. Six-foot-three and a tad burly, with reading glasses forever perched on the tip of his nose, he had a quiet, imposing "don't mess with me" attitude. About 60 years of age, he gave off the air of a man who had been around the block—one you did not want to mess with.

Then there was his sinister-looking Italian gentleman friend in his black two-piece suits. He always showed up at the agency unannounced. No one really spoke with him except my boss. They would both go into his office and have quiet meetings. Rumor had it that he was in the Mafia. I learned early on to be polite and nothing else. Whenever they both were in the agency offices, I would say my "Good morning," "Good evening," or "Hello" and move on back to my desk

Now, on the first day of running my own agency, Bill was calmly telling me to "shut it down and come back to work with him or he would break…" You get the point. I had seen *Scarface*, *The Godfather* and just about every mob movie ever made before I came to America, and now, in my mind, I was starring in a real life Mafia drama called *My Ex-Boss Is a Mobster*. But this was no movie. It was real.

Well, I wasn't going back to his agency. I knew better than to return and face him.

After he had diplomatically made his points and informed me that he knew exactly where my office was, he calmly said goodbye and hung up. I sat, holding the phone in my hand, shaking. My dream of owning my own *Vogue* agency was off to a rocky start.

I rushed to the door of my 200-square foot office and bolted it. The bathroom was down the hall, but going to the bathroom didn't seem as important now as keeping my possibly murderous ex-boss on the other side of that door. I prayed: "Lord, help me to get through this!"

Next, I had to tell Andrew, a former model who also ran cheese stores in the East Village and Brooklyn, that I was about to book an airline ticket and catch the next flight out of New York. Jamaica or London seemed far enough away to be safe.

I called Andrew and told him about my conversation with Bill. He laughed. The more we talked about the call, the better I felt. We were scared as two church mice in a kitchen pantry when the lights came on, but we both kept laughing. The whole thing was just so ridiculous!

There were two choices: close the agency or keep it open. With Andrew's encouragement, I decided I was not going anywhere. The agency would stay open. Of course, I had another problem: I had to go home. That meant that I had to leave the safety of my locked office.

I was scared to open the door, fearing that my ex-boss would be waiting outside with a baseball bat, ready to shatter my kneecaps and then every other body part, as he'd promised he would. I could see the headline in the *New York Post*: "Fashion agent bludgeoned to death by ex-boss!"

I prayed...and then I called a photographer friend named Ken 'Kenny' Grey and asked him to come and meet me that evening so that I would not have to walk the long stretch from Eleventh Avenue all the way up to Eighth to catch the train alone. Ken found the whole thing amusing, which made me laugh even more—that nervous kind of laughter that makes you cackle even louder.

Every morning and evening for about two weeks, I prayed that my vengeful former boss wouldn't meet me at the corner and kneecap me for leaving his agency. At the end of the day, I had Kenny meet me so that I would have someone to walk with (as a witness, just in case) to the station or just to a cafe to get a cup of tea and pecan pie. Every other day, like clockwork, Bill would call to remind me that he was, as he put it, "watching me." Sometimes, his Joan Collins-esque former secretary—who I had trained to be an agent and who had replaced me when I left—would call and say, "We're going to get you."

With all this supposed surveillance going on, lunch outside of the office was out of the question. I got delivery from local delis daily. I hated going to the office; I dreaded Bill and his cohorts being there and something going terribly wrong. The only way I could go to the toilet was to run straight there while looking over my shoulder. It was terrible.

But after about two weeks of the constant threats, I stopped being scared and started to become really annoyed. It had to stop. I had to decide who my "agent" was, and I knew it wasn't my former boss. I had to stand firm on the Lord's word that He would be my shepherd and face my Goliath ex-boss like David the psalmist did when he defeated the Philistine with nothing more than a slingshot and a few stones.

I didn't have a sling to use on Bill, but I had my mouth. For a long time, I had prayed to God to help me keep my mouth shut. But now I said, "Lord, help me. This time, I need to keep my big mouth open!"

I still wasn't dumb enough to meet him face-to-face, and I didn't need to. The next day, he called and made the usual threats. But this time, I was ready. After he had finished, I calmly said, "Everything you just said has been recorded by the NYPD and the FBI."

Click. The line went dead. I never received a call from Bill or Joan Collins again. I'd slain Goliath with the power of my mouth. The Lord is not only my shepherd but my agent, and because he has given me my *Vogue* dream, there will always be someone trying to kill it before it even comes true. But I can stand up to the Goliaths (fashionistas and ex-bosses), face them head-on and slay them with the words from God.

This is my story of faith, hard work, prayer and love that transcends all boundaries, and the Agent who guides our lives daily.

"Let Jesus alone be seen and glorified in the pages of this book. Let all praise and glory go to Him, for He is the true author and agent of my life."

Part One

LIFE LESSONS

One

JAMAICA

Not only did I not dream of being a modeling agent when I was growing up in Jamaica, I had no idea that there was such a profession. But I was a dreamer. I was the second of six children, and my parents were not conventional: they did not live together under the same roof all their lives. My mom lived part of the time with her parents, part of the time with our dad.

My father was a printer who worked for the government, so at an early age I had a lot of knowledge of the printing industry. My father also ran a printing office in the yard of our home and would take on books that needed restoration. He was a genius at restoring all sorts of books. He would take my older brother's tattered schoolbooks (he was one year ahead of me in school) and bind them back together until they looked brand new for me to take to school the following year. His last project before he died was an old bible he was restoring for a local lady. He would joke to me that he should just buy her a brand new one since it was so badly damaged, but he knew that the old pages meant a great deal to her, so he kept working on it.

Because of my father, I loved books. They became part of my life's escape.

My mother was a dressmaker and the hardest working person I ever met. I can't ever remember her sleeping or taking a nap. As far as I know, she never stopped working. She would travel for miles by land, air, or sea to make sure she finished whatever she was working on. She would sew all hours of the day and straight into the night without stopping. If I woke up at 3 a.m. I could guarantee that she would still be at it.

Every day at 6 a.m. (especially on the weekends), she would have her bags packed, ready to go to the markets to sell her dresses. During the recession and political upheaval of the 1970s, many families got hit hard—including ours. Because of this, my mom would travel to other countries such as Canada and Panama to buy clothes and household products that she could bring back to Jamaica and sell in the markets in order to keep food on our table. She hated to disappoint anyone, even if it meant her health or traveling thousands of miles. She was not afraid of taking chances. She knew that God would always provide for her and our family so she always made sure to give God thanks for everything.

From her, I learned if I trusted in God in times of trouble, I wouldn't have to fear anything.

My grandparents on my mom's side were always with us. We actually lived with them whenever we were not at my dad's home. My mother took care of them and wanted to be near them at all times. My big brother and I developed a daily routine: delivering dinner to our father's house each evening. My father, for his part, hated this arrangement; he and my mother would argue many times over her need to live with her parents. But as the years went by, it became normal, and my father would glow with happiness whenever one of his children was around to spend the day or night with him.

My grandfather, Dillon, was a beautiful man with wavy silver hair, grey/hazel eyes, and a perpetual smile. He was a dapper fashion plate at all times, unquestionably a gentleman. His suits were always crisp and sharply ironed. As a teenager, I would sneak into his closet and borrow his polished shoes and his slick trousers to wear to a social occasion. If I did this on a Saturday night, he might get upset when he checked his closet to choose the suit he would wear to church the next day only to find it missing. But secretly, I think he was happy knowing that I was wearing his clothes and dressing like a gentleman.

He also loved going to church and praising God. His hope was that I would become a minister but God knew best. I'm sure God remembered my grandfather's desire and put me in a position to have a ministry of sorts in the fashion industry. One thing is for sure: God has a sense of humor.

My grandmother—we called her Ma May, because she was born in the month of May—was a quiet, beautifully calm lady, yet very stern. She said little but she would always give us a hug or have a little talk with us in a corner. When she was angry, then we would hear it!

Ma May loved her garden, especially her roses. Each morning she would be up early to water her plants, checking to see all the different variations of roses or flowers that had bloomed overnight. In the backyard, she had her vegetable garden: ripe red tomatoes, okra, peas and whatever else she would plant. It was a joy for her to pick the fruits of her labor. I loved my granny, and I loved her rose garden. It was a place for me to sit and dream.

Then there were the strangers she would take in. Ma May took in total strangers who had nowhere to go, and in order not to wound their pride, she would offer them a job as our nanny or "helper," especially when our mom was away in another country. We would come home from school and find someone we did not know moving in or eating a meal. We never really needed a nanny or servant, but Ma May refused to turn anyone away—especially if they needed a bed to sleep in or food to eat.

Her kindness to strangers inspired me to do the same for others when I was older. She taught me to remember that we were blessed and that one of us could easily have been the poor soul without food, clothes or a roof over his head. In other words, we learned to walk in other people's shoes and understand what they were going through.

My grandparents, especially my grandfather, knew I was going places far beyond his imagination. He predicted it, and I believed it. By the time I became a successful agent, I had already lived in London, Munich and New York City and was shuttling back and forth between Paris, London, Milan and every other major fashion capitol. Sadly, my grandfather did not live to see all this; he died just after I moved back to America from England. Ma May was proud that I was working but never actually understood what I did. She couldn't have cared less what a model agent did. Her only concern was that I was serving God and talking to Him daily.

Thank God for grandparents. Thank God for their predictions and their prayers. My future in the fashion industry was probably made inevitable by my parents and grandparents: my father working in the printing industry, my mom being a dressmaker, my grandmother tending her rose garden and my grandfather's dapper sense of fashion.

Don't Worry, Be Happy, Give Us Your Money

Life was not perfect on the island, but it was always interesting. Jamaica is a wonderful example of the beauty of God's handiwork. I grew up surrounded by crystal clear turquoise waters and lush forests filled with the flavors of fruits and vegetables perfect for whetting one's appetite. The succulent taste of jerk chicken, marinated with the seasonings and spices brought to the island throughout the centuries from Africa, India and China, made the aroma of Jamaican cuisine a joy to the senses. The people are as pungent as the spices: cool as cucumbers, sweet as ripe mangoes, but also as hot (in temperament) as scorching scotch bonnet peppers.

The island was, and is, a religious and cultural melting pot: churches, synagogues, temples, revivals, pocomanias, evangelicals and everything else, including the cool, weed-smoking Rastafarians who the elite, educated Jamaicans always looked down upon, populated the island. Everyone seemed to be a minister, politician, an actor or an athlete—some more than one at the same time. This is the same island where Bob Marley sang that everything was "Irie," "no problem," and to "don't worry about a thing..."

I grew up knowing that "every little thing is going to be alright" was not the way things really were. So it was not that surprising when one night around 10:30, in my final year at high school, after I left my best friend Gary's home (where we had celebrated his sister Kathy's birthday) a few blocks away in the quiet residential suburb of my grandparents, two men with stockings over their heads came out of the woods and stuck a gun in my face and told me to "Walk straight ahead into the ravine of the woods" that separated the local college from the luxury homes in the community called Ravina.

Scared was not the word to describe the feeling that swept over me. I had never been in such a situation before. Held up? Yes, that was part of living in a place where poverty and riches existed side by side. But I had never been held up by masked men and led into the bushes.

All I had were two slices of Kathy's birthday cake and a few dollars in my pocket.

It was normal for me to walk at all hours of the day or night, even though my mom had warned me not to do so since there had been an increase in robberies and hold-ups in the neighborhood recently. I was never afraid; "don't worry" was my mantra, like Marley. After all, I had God on my side!

The other times I had been held up during the school year had been on the buses. Gunmen or "rude boys" would get on the buses posing as normal passengers. Generally, they worked in groups of two or three: one would sit near the driver's seat while the rest sat throughout the bus. When they were ready, one would hold a gun or knife to the bus driver's head to force him to stop while the others took wallets from the passengers. When the bus stopped, they would take their loot and scamper off into the dark.

But this time I was not on a bus with other people. I was alone. Unlike on the bus, where I could be inconspicuous because I was small, I was the target, being led into the bushes. They marched me into the woods and told me to lie face down on the wet grass. Of course, I obeyed. They took the bag with the two slices of cake, then went through my pockets and took the few dollars I had. Then no one said anything, while I laid face down on the damp grass, praying harder than I had in my entire life.

After ten or fifteen minutes lying face down, pleading for them to let me go, I heard nothing. I thought that they might have left; I had not heard because I had been praying so loudly. It's strange how we think when we're in dire situations.

Slowly, I lifted my head up from the dewy grass only to hear one of them say, "He's seen our face, shoot him!" I felt sure I was going to wet myself. I fell back to the ground face-first as one of the guys took the gun and pressed it against my face. I cried "Don't shoot! I didn't see your face!" The one with the gun seemed ready to shoot me, while the other stood quietly, not saying much. I prayed and pleaded with them for mercy.

After what seemed like hours, one of them said, "Quiet—shut up!"

The other said, "Get up, don't look back and run fast!"

Run I did—straight home, not looking back! Olympic gold medal sprinter Usain Bolt had nothing on me that night!

"No problem," "don't worry, be happy," and "Irie, mon" did not matter to me then, but throughout my life, they would come to matter much more than the fear I had felt that night.

Two

OPENING MY EYES TO BEAUTY

*L*ife in Jamaica wasn't always easy, but it was there, in that sensual place, that I first became aware of the beauty that God placed within the human form. Strangely, I learned about it from the "potheads."

Gary was my best friend in school; Paul was his brother. Both were potheads. They smoked Jamaican weed, the best in the world. At least, that's what the foreigners and the Jamaicans would say, even though most Jamaicans do not smoke marijuana. In fact, it is frowned upon and considered lower class to do so.

But Gary and Paul were not lower class. They were from a "fine" family, as most Jamaicans described people who've achieved wealth or grew up with privilege. They were "Irie cool," and I loved hanging with them, especially since Gary and I went to the same high school and lived only a few blocks from each other. Gary was cool and good-looking, and the girls loved him. He was quiet and reserved, but I think that was more due to the joints he would smoke daily than to his true nature.

He would laugh, "A pot a day keeps Gary away...from school that is!" He would often be so high that he would sleep through the day and miss his classes.

I wasn't the only one hanging out at Gary's parents home after school. We had a little social circle: Steve Ying, a Chinese Jamaican kid; Melton and Cassetta Chin, who were also of Chinese descent (Cassetta was drop-dead beautiful with her Farrah Fawcett hairstyle);

and Selena, who must have been of Syrian or Indian descent. She was the sexiest of them all and the most sought-after girl in school. We were all best friends.

Gary's house was our usual meeting spot where we would play table tennis or Pac Man or just roll joints for Gary or Paul. By age 14, I had become an expert roller. Gary would weed out the seeds and I would roll that smooth white paper until everything was perfectly coifed. Then I would lick it gently (not too much moisture) so that it would stick together perfectly. Strangely, though, I was never interested in smoking cigarettes or pot, even though there's an abundance of it on the island. To this day, I have never smoked marijuana in Jamaica.

Selena had dropped out of high school during her final year for what seemed like a few months, but the day she showed up outside the school, I knew I was looking at my future. I saw her coming down the street before she saw me. She and Cassetta were walking together, and you could not miss them. With long wild curly hair, full lips painted cherry-red from the lipstick she wore, with perfect pearly white teeth that shone like the noonday sun against her tanned Mediterranean skin, Selena was impossible not to look at. She reminded me more of a young Elizabeth Taylor than a model; that's how beautiful she was.

Cassetta, with her big Farah Fawcett hairdo and curvy body to die for, was equally stunning. While Selena had the long legs of a giraffe, Cassetta had a body made for sin. Women hated them both, especially when men were around. They were beautiful creatures from another planet, and they knew how to have fun. Men young and old loved them. They all wanted Selena, but sweet, pot-smoking Gary was the one that got her. That just shows you that sometimes, it's not about how you look or what you do, but the soul inside you.

God definitely got it right when He made beautiful women...and men!

I found out later that when Selena had left school, she had come back as a supermodel in training. I felt like Charlie and they my angels;

they were my first ideals of models. That was the first time I knew I wanted to work in an industry with beauties like these. But I had no idea how! I did know that it was not going to happen on an island as small as Jamaica. But I was going to do something great in fashion as soon as school was out. I was going to manage beautiful people, and Selena and Cassetta were going to be my inspiration.

And pot smoking Gary, too.

Dear Janet...

Growing up, I hadn't dreamed of becoming an agent for fashion models. I thought I'd get into management or become a journalist or reporter in the entertainment world. I saw myself being behind the scenes, never in front of the camera. Maybe I would be an entertainment manager taking care of beautiful people like Selena and Cassetta, who had every eye glued to them as they sauntered along the road.

I thought being in front of a camera was a bit vulgar and arrogant even though I loved looking at *Vogue* and reading other fashion magazines. That changed when I got to know Janet. She was an "advice to the lovelorn" columnist in the manner of "Dear Abby" in the United States.

Janet was a celebrity known for giving advice to anyone who asked or wrote in about relationships. Her column was syndicated both in England and Canada. But Janet was not an ordinary advice writer; she was a businesswoman. Like many Jamaicans, she had her hands in many pots—and that included running a few beauty pageants.

A zaftig woman, Janet was one of a kind. She would arm herself daily with rolls of coins and take to the streets in a chauffeured taxi, headed for one of her "offices"—local telephone company pay phones. To these phones she would bring her slippers, a bag of coins, and a tattered, manhandled Yellow Pages phone book with markings all over the pages. No client list, Rolodex or fancy gadgets with names of her top clients. No plush, deluxe office space in a luxury building for Janet. Just the Yellow Pages. All her clients were listed there, and she would work those directories over and over until they fell apart. Then she would simply get a new one. Her hired taxi driver's main job was to deliver pageant tickets to clients, pick up checks and take the checks back to Janet.

If you were nearby when she was working, you would hear the sounds of coins tinkling in the pay phone as she dialed the presidents and CEOs of major corporations. In a charmingly delicate, smooth and proper phone voice, she would purr her familiar, "Hello, this is Janet from..." or whatever alias she was using that day. Every word rolled off her lips like a delicious piece of Jamaican rum cake topped with frosted lemon icing. Like a rich socialite or an Oxford professor, she would charm the trousers (or skirts) off them—especially if the person was a man, which she always preferred.

Janet was no "street business woman" at a pay phone; she was an educated and intelligent woman and could run rings around her suitors. With charm alone, she would sway a man into forking out hundreds or thousands of dollars for tickets to attend one of her events that he would rarely ever attend. She was especially effective when she used her spiel about "part of the ticket sales going to charity." She always did give to charity, just not as much as those CEOs believed. Her favorite charity was herself.

Janet was the first real marketer and salesperson I ever saw. I was amazed at how she could sell 99 percent of her tickets to those high-powered executives without paying a dime for advertising space in newspapers. Watching her, I saw the power of using charm in marketing on the phone without ever having to meet the client face to face. It was the best training for a future would-be model manager. Janet gave me my first lesson in the power of marketing. I knew that when I began to build my career, I was going to emulate everything I saw Janet do in building her client roster. I would use those tools at every modeling management company or entertainment firm.

Janet taught me so much just by example. Her first lesson: *Focus*.

As she stood in her phone booths, cars would be roaring by, but Janet did not hear them. No matter who she was speaking to, she knew when to put her hands on the mouthpiece to block out any traffic noise that would interfere with her conversation. In those days, there were no Starbucks to sit at with laptops, you know! But Janet had mastered the art of not paying for high-end real estate space. Why should she, when the public phones would do just as well?

It was tacky but ingenious. I can only imagine the looks on the faces of some of those captains of industry if they'd known that the smooth, charismatic woman on the other end of the line was talking to them from a pay phone.

Janet's next lesson: *Early to rise.*

An early bird, she was eager to get as many "worms" as possible. I don't think she ever left her phone booths until she had sold a few thousand dollars worth of tickets at $25 or $30 each. By the end of most days, she was smiling as widely as the Cheshire cat.

Janet's third lesson: *Delegate.*

Once her deals were done, she would have her chauffeured taxi driver (she never took public transportation) go with one of her assistants (she generally had one or two people whose job was to hang around her pay phone all day long waiting to see what chores she had for them) to deliver the tickets she had sold, which were always neatly placed in an envelope and carefully labeled as if they were being delivered to an embassy.

I assisted her as best I could and loved every minute of it. She was the first "beauty agent" I ever witnessed. I was an apprentice learning from the best. Janet was amazing. I was a sponge, trying to learn as much as possible from her. She didn't pay me, but being around her and learning from her were much more valuable to me than money.

I say today that I graduated from the University of Janet, *summa cum laude* in a class of one.

Leaving Home

Since I wasn't the typical high school student, graduation day was the most exciting of my life. I could not wait for the sermon to be over. Forgive me, Father. While my classmates were crying their little hearts out and talking about how much they were going to miss each other, I kept thinking, "I'm out of here!"

It was time for me to leave my beautiful little island and settle elsewhere. I had my heart set on working in the entertainment or fashion industries and knew that wasn't going to happen if I stayed on Jamaica. I had outgrown the place where I was born, and I knew that God had put the desire in my heart to get up and go to a place that He would show me, just like he did with Abraham. I had fulfilled my parent's dreams of completing high school by passing my exams in the English school system.

Now, with my cap and gown on, I couldn't wait to get out. I was headed to a different island: *Manhattan*. I had now met quite a number of international fashion models—including Iman and Mounia, two of Yves Saint Laurent's biggest models—when they made appearances on separate shows where I had offered to work backstage for free. I was fearless: I would ask them questions and they would talk about their agents and what kind of work they were doing. Each time I would get more excited to hear their stories of bookings and travels to exotic places.

I was determined to learn the business of managing people in fashion, but I had no idea exactly how or where I was going to do it. I knew I was never going to be a designer, model, or stylist, but I definitely saw myself working on the business side of "the business." Like Abraham, I was not going to be content being on a small island when the world was bigger than my eyes could see or imagine. I was going to trust the Lord as he did and pack my bags, get up, and trust God to lead the way.

As a child I had an imaginative and active mind, and I would dream of what I was going to become one day. My dreams became more concrete when I discovered author Harold Robbins and his glamorous book, *The Carpetbaggers*. It soon became my favorite reading, along with *Vogue*; when it became a movie, I sneaked into the theatre to see it. *The Carpetbaggers* opened my eyes to a world of incredible glamour, wealth and beauty, and the rich and famous—something I had never seen but now couldn't stop imagining.

I had read Shakespeare, which was mandatory for English Literature in school, but as a teenager *The Carpetbaggers* transported me to a new world that was different and exciting.

While in school I had done some assistant work with a producer who had brought The Commodores to Jamaica to perform, so I had a little taste for how the rich and famous lived their lives—chic yet dangerous. Needless to say, Mr. Robbins and his book would be joining me—along with my Bible and the story of Abraham—as I journeyed in faith, with God leading the way to whatever that may be.

Three

MODELS FOR CHRIST

*W*hile I was learning how to be a "street agent" from Janet, I took notes. Nothing I learned later would prove more valuable. But during my last years in Jamaica I also met Brian, a school portrait photographer who got me into being a "jet setter." This was the closest I was going to get to my dreams of the fashion world for a while, and I ate it up.

Brian hired me to get his school photos processed. I would fly back and forth to New York, Chicago, Boston—anywhere in the world as long as I was able to get his film processed and return the finished products to him so that he could make sure every school principal got their packages of finished portraits. I did not have to pay for any of these trips, but Brian made sure I took a few cases of Overproof Jamaican rum to give to his clients to cover their costs. It wasn't unusual for me to fly to New York, get film done in a day or two and then head back to the island.

What a way to start a fashion career!

It was simple, especially for a high school student, since I would leave either on a Friday evening or Saturday morning and be back home by Sunday night. I also got to see the beautiful city of New York in all its glory. I got a free airline ticket and hotel. I wasn't being paid (maybe $100 in spending money) but who cared? I would have paid Brian just to let me travel. It was during one of these trips—on a Saturday afternoon in New York—that I was walking past the entrance of Central Park at 59th and Columbus Circle when

I heard the most amazing voices sweetly singing songs of praise to God.

As I stopped to listen, the choir of ten or twelve men and women, young and old, sang so wonderfully that my heart melted in that one moment. I felt the love for God engulf my entire being.

A young blonde man in his late twenties or early thirties came over and introduced himself and talked to me about the Lord. Then he asked me something that took me utterly by surprise. He said, "Are you in the fashion or entertainment industry?" Without thinking twice, I told him I was going to be an agent for models. The words rolled off my tongue like butter on white toast.

The meditation of my heart had spilled out, and I had finally spoken the words that I had been unable to put together for so long. The man, Luke, smiled and told me of an organization that fashion models and industry folks, who were also born-again Christians, attended. It was called "Models for Christ," a name that intrigued me even more.

There are Christians in fashion, I thought. This was thrilling. I thought I was going to have to walk amongst the "shadows of death" in fashion without any godly guidance or support. But here was Luke telling me that there were others like me in the industry who were seeking and proclaiming the Lord! I was elated. My family would be proud, knowing that I would still seek the Lord in an industry that was better known for worshipping the flesh, material wealth and pride.

Luke told me of a little church he attended that a number of models and Broadway actors also attended. They would worship on Sunday morning and on Wednesday hold a prayer meeting called Unbroken Chain. Luke took my number, and later he called to invite me to church.

Like many in Jamaica, I was brought up in an Anglican Church, known elsewhere as the Episcopal Church. My grandfather always wanted me to become a minister, but instead I ended up chasing the beauty of what he called "frock tails & trousers." I knew as a child how important it was to love the Lord and worship Him with all my heart, so faith wasn't anything foreign to me. But the sermon I heard that Sunday morning in New York was different and totally beautiful. The preacher was a little lady by the name of Pastor Maria, and she held the audience spellbound.

I looked around at the attendees. In one corner of the church was John DeLorean, the former super car builder who was going through prosecution for drug trafficking. In another corner, with her hands raised praising God, was Coco Mitchell, a top *Sports Illustrated* model who I recognized from the magazines. All around the sanctuary were different shades, colors and sizes of people doing the same thing: praising and worshipping God!

That was the day I gave my heart to the Lord.

It was like meeting the love of your life for the first time, even though I had talked to Him before on many occasions. You know in your heart that the person is "The One." That's what it was like with the Lord and me. It was a love that would take me far and wide, a love that would travel with me everywhere I went. Even when I betrayed Him and stole kisses here and there with others, in His loving mercy and kindness He would always hold His arms wide open ready to take me back.

I was a serial cheater, and He was a forgiving lover.

Pretty People

The next time I was back in town, Luke asked me to attend a Models for Christ meeting at the home of Linda and James, two top models who were engaged. There, I met other fashion industry folks from models and stylists to photographers. There I was introduced to Kathy Ireland, who was a sweetheart: incredibly kind and very beautiful.

Surprisingly, there was no ego amongst the attendees. This made it comfortable for me—a newcomer who had accomplished nothing—to interact. The amazing thing, however, was that nobody was networking. I loved it. We were there just to worship and praise God, and that, to me, was how it was supposed to be.

One day, my photographer friend Kenny introduced me to a small agency named Pretty People. Previously, I had met Gail Morris from the Elite model agency after telling myself that I would only work with the best. Why not? Gail was incredibly kind. Despite the fact that her agency was not looking for anyone at that moment, she sat me down and gave me a large set of composite photo cards of all their models—including their stars—and told me to study the images and the style of the photographers and come back in a few months.

I left in awe that I had actually met someone from one of the most prestigious agencies in New York. I was sure that I would come back in a few months and be offered a job on the spot. But, fate took over with Ken's introduction to Pretty People Models. It wasn't Elite, but I was eager to learn. What better place to learn than the bottom?

There, a funny little man from Poland with a big heart by the name of Roland, and his wife, Mary, immediately took a liking to me and offered me a job as an agent. They were the blessing that God used to give me my start in New York.

Roland loved short models. "Pygmies," he'd call them.

I thought, *My God, what am I going to do with pygmies? I want Vogue!*

But Roland loved his pygmies, and every Monday morning he would come in with another one of his from Long Island so that I could make models out of them. I learnt an important lesson then and there: do the best you can with what you have, be thankful, and don't complain.

I had no clue what I was doing, so I relied on my lessons from Janet. I recalled the way she would work the phones, getting people on her side and buying tickets from her. However, this time I was not on a street corner, and there was no chauffeur-driven taxi driver to help me. I was on my own. I wasn't delivering tickets; I was delivering flesh to clients paying big bucks for my models to sell their products. I was a Christian working in the flesh business, praising God at the same time. It was a little unusual. However, I knew that God was directing my steps, so I wasn't really doing it on my own.

I decided that I was going to be polite, nice and an example of Christianity in the industry. I was going to be myself, which is a radical move in a business where everybody is always trying to be someone else. I thought about what Janet would have done and did it. I was charming and considerate and nice.

Amazingly, it worked. Clients started calling back on nearly every call. Bookings came in for the few tall models we represented and even for Roland's lovely little "pygmies." After a while Roland introduced me to an Italian agent by the name of Paolo. For some reason, he saw potential in me and immediately offered me a job: come to Milan and work in his agency.

I could barely stay upright. I was going to go to Milan! I was entering the jet set. I was going to become an Italian-speaking international agent.

Jet Setter

I had family in England, and I had overstayed my visa in the United States, so I went to the UK and waited for Paolo to call. And he did. But each time, he had a different excuse as to why I couldn't come to Milan yet. My jet setting wasn't going quite as I had hoped.

Meanwhile, I was bored. I was hanging out at my Uncle Roy and Aunt Fay's four-bedroom attached house in London, with its separate sitting room and living room, having cups upon cups of tea and hoping one day to play the piano that stood in the sitting room. My cousin Judy, who was about twelve years old at the time, loved having me around. Her sister Brigitte and I had grown up together; Brigitte was older than I and had become a Jehovah's Witness walking the streets of London sharing the gospel. Her other sister Debbie was also out of the house, probably at University or living with her future husband.

I was still a young adult, so hanging with Judy was cool. She soaked up all my stories about New York, God, Jamaica, and so on. I loved Judy; she was quiet and serene like an angel come down from heaven to remind us how pure and simple life can be. When I heard a few years later that she passed away far too young, I thought, *She always belonged in Heaven.*

Anyway, while waiting to hear from Paolo, I met a number of Germans in London. We would hang out and chat and laugh together. But when they learned that I was waiting to hear from my mysterious Italian benefactor, they all started saying the same thing: "Go to Germany instead. You'll love it there!"

I'd never thought about Germany before. I was a fashion person, and the only places we went were New York, Paris, London and Milan. Anything else was passé, or so I thought.

Like migrating geese, fashion folks move into these cities each season, their bodies covered head to toe in black and dark shades, jumping out of chauffeured black sedans, waiting for the seas of onlookers to part like the Red Sea so that they can blow air kisses to each other with one eye closed and the other opened just to see exactly who has noticed. Then they smile their very important smiles and say "Hello, darling!"

Then the scene moves inside cramped show tents, where fights for front row seats are common. Even the "commoners" try to look important before an audience of their peers, with everyone acting as if the world is about to end unless they are seated in the front row. They are a truly special breed of people with serious mental disabilities. I have never understood the concept of wearing black day in, day out, as if you're always ready to go to a funeral, but it's the uniform of the Fashion People.

That's the way I think now. But back then, young and naïve, I had the sense that I should learn to dress like everyone, wear black every day and blow fancy kisses on both cheeks that never touched, wink with one eye and hold my head high in the air with a sense of superiority. Anything else was passé, including Germany.

But I was ready to get out of dreary England and find a greener pasture that was a little closer to Milan, where I wanted to be. So after waiting long enough for the call that would summon me to Italy, I took the plunge and went to the British Airways office to get a ticket to Germany. One of my friends said if I went to Munich he would hook me up with an apartment that one of his clients had.

The only words I knew in German were "nein" and "ja." Now, I was going to learn to "sprachen sie Deutsch" whether I liked it or not.

Without anyone to meet me at the airport, I learned how to navigate around the city, reading the long German words, and finally made it to the apartment. I noticed the church across the street and knew that was a good sign. Like Abraham, I was on a journey to a place I had no clue about. In Genesis 12, God had not told him where he was going, but Abraham believed and went. Now I was following in his faith and footsteps, sojourning in a land unbeknownst to me. I could have stayed in London and tried to find a job there, but now I was in a beautiful land and was going to enjoy the milk and honey to be found here...I hoped.

It didn't take me long to meet Boris and his friends, who I was to share the apartment with. They were pot smokers, which made me feel right at home. They were friends of the son of the man who owned the apartment. The son must have been a teen idol or something at one point; the apartment was filled with magazines that bore pictures of him and his name, Daniel. When I spoke with them, I found out that the apartment was their main hangout spot after school. They would come and smoke their joints or cigarettes and drink beers.

Dear God, I'm a Christian, I thought. *Why am I being followed by pot smokers?*

Then again, Christ chilled out with drunks, whoremongers and the lot and ministered to them. Why not me? Anyway, beggars can't be choosers.

Everyone loved that I was Jamaican. Some people see something mystical in where I come from. I have no clue what it is. In any case, my new pot-smoking buddies were really cool; they would stay in one room while I relaxed in mine. So it took me a while to realize that the neighborhood I lived in was so chic and rich. For example, the large three-bedroom apartment was right beside a lake with swans and...a palace! It was the Nymphenburg, one of the most magical and beautiful gardens in Europe. It was like I was living a Hans Christian Andersen's fairy tale in real life, for free!

My God, you took me from little Jamaica to live beside a palace in Germany? Praise the Lord! I thought about Paolo. God bless him, he gave me a great gift by delaying my trip.

German Lessons

I made the most of my days by picking up newspapers and trying to read German or just enjoying the beauty of my surroundings. But after getting used to the customs for a few weeks and spending time roaming the palace grounds watching the tourists, I knew it was time to get a job. My destiny to get into the fashion industry would come when God saw fit, in Milan or somewhere else. In the meantime, I needed to eat.

I knew it was easier to work in a restaurant and work your way up. I got a job working as a waiter in a bar/restaurant. They all loved me for being Jamaican. The manager, patrons and other waiters would ask me to sing some Bob Marley songs, but no one had warned them how bad a singer I was. I politely tried to sing a few bars, but thank God there are not many high notes in any of Marley's songs. The patrons loved me, too, and I enjoyed serving them—except when meine Deutsch would get all mixed up and I would say something ridiculous like "Do you want eggs with your locomotive?" Then the giggles would start. I laughed too; this was the best training I could get, making mistakes and learning from them.

But I started to get lonely. I was learning to speak a new language, but I had no close friends around. I looked forward to my weekly phone calls to my family.

Then Molly appeared. She was a tall blonde from California who was now living in Hamburg. I had been Molly's agent at Pretty People, and we had formed a close friendship. She was one of the few models at Roland's agency who stood over 5'9". I had called her the girl with the "tall blonde hair" when we worked together, and the nickname stuck with her. She moved to Hamburg to work, but after a few months without much work she had gained some weight and her agency put her on a diet. Bored and in different cities, we chatted on the phone daily.

Then the Lord sent an angel in the form of a model named Maxine Winters. She was a Jamaican model I had represented at Pretty People and had done well in New York. She was tall, tanned and amazing to behold, with a baby doll face to go with a divine body. My heart jumped when I saw her picture in the papers even though she was wearing a fur hat and jacket and was flanked by two blonde models and the designer. I read in haste, found the designer's name, scanned the phone book for his number, dialed it and told my story: I was Maxine's agent from New York, now living in Germany, and would they please forward her my number?

Unbeknownst to me, Molly had gone to a fashion show that same day and saw Maxine sauntering down the catwalk. I couldn't wait for Molly to come home to tell her the good news that Maxine was in Germany—and likewise, she couldn't wait to do the same! God was clearly working by connecting us all at the same time.

We met Maxine later that day and had a joyful reunion. She was doing great in Germany and was as beautiful and sweet as I remembered. Because our funds were so low, she was a lifesaver; on many a day she would put 50 or 100 deutschmarks in our pockets just to make sure Molly and I were okay. However, I will always remember the blessing of her spicy Jamaican curried chicken with hot white rice, so fragrant that you could smell it all the way down at the train station along the tram lines of Munich. It was audaciously sinful.

Then one day, Maxine introduced me to Odessa, owner of Odessa Models. She offered me the opportunity to scout for her, but that was a problem. I was now living in the woods far outside of Munich, and without a car, I had no way to commute back into the city. I spent a few weeks riding bicycles in the woods with Molly and doing little else. It was terrible. I was no longer in the city in my own room; I was sleeping on a sofa while Molly slept like a lamb in the bedroom with her sweetheart. Even worse, I was missing out on a modeling industry opportunity.

After a few weeks I decided I was going back to London. I never did make it to Milan.

Four

LONDON CALLING

*T*his time in London, I was not going to make the same mistakes. I wouldn't stay at my Uncle Roy's house with my lovely cousin Judy. It was time to either find a proper job or go back to school.

First, I found a place to live at the home of a friend who was an antique dealer: a large triplex on Shakespeare Road in Brixton. Later I moved into my Uncle Alan's home in Leytonstone. That was one important item off my list.

Next: a job. I decided to do whatever I could to get a job with a modeling agency. I wasn't ready to give up my dream. A friend introduced me to Valerie, an English-born agent of Jamaican and German descent. She immediately told me I could come in and learn the business through her agency, V, whenever I wanted to. I accepted on the spot. It was a dream come true: I was going to be a junior agent in London!

I loved that Valerie's agency was so different from all the other agencies that I had seen in London. I had met June Glastonbury, one of the owners of a top London agency, and her girls were typical "English roses": rosy cheeks, demure and fragile, like modern-day versions of a character from Jane Austen novels. Such girls were a dime a dozen in Great Britain, so they did not stand out.

V was the exact opposite. This was the height of the punk rock era in London, and it seemed that Valerie had every extreme-looking model in the industry on her books. More important, her models were all *working*—and working high-profile jobs. They were in the top fashion magazines, including *ID* and *The Face,* and in every major designer show in Paris and London. Valerie was also representing some of London's top fashion photographers. It was a fantastic place to learn the business from both a modeling and photography perspective.

Amanda, one of V's agents, was the best agent I had ever met. She had a bottomless supply of adjectives to describe her models that were guaranteed to make an impression: "Darling, she's such a lovely English Rose…" "She's like a daffodil on a dark, gloomy day…" "She's like a gentle cup of tea on a cold, dreary day…!" And she meant every word. She really cared about her girls.

Amanda was a "nutter" and a genius. She got all the top bookings in the city. So I sat close, listened, and watched everything she did, just as I had with Janet in her phone booth back in Jamaica. She was the best, and I wanted to learn from her. I started emulating her style by adding my own island flavor—along with bits of Janet's wisdom—whenever I would call clients.

One day, Amanda told me the story of how one of our models had left the agency. The model had come in while we were in the office and sweetly asked for her portfolios. She'd put them in a bag, flashed her pearly whites, and purred, "I love you all, but I've got to go!" She then swept out the door charmingly and gracefully, just as a true English lady would. It was only after she'd gone that everyone else realized that she was leaving the agency and that we would no longer be representing her.

The story itself was funny, but Amanda made it hilarious and comical with her perfect impression of the model's mannerisms and voice. That was "Mad Amanda": she could take something serious and make us all laugh at it and realize it was part of life!

Personally, I never forgot the line, "I love you all, but I've got to go!" I hoped that one day I would be able to use it myself as I made my own dramatic exit.

Will Humiliate Self for Money

I was learning every day, but working at the agency meant that I was also making very little money. It was a boutique agency, and since I was the new kid on the block I had to prove my worth first before earning a pound…or even a penny.

To supplement my income, I went looking for a job in a restaurant. In Leicester Square in the heart of London, I heard about the opening of a hip new French restaurant with the unlikely name of Bill Stickers, where everyone had to wear chic French uniforms. I applied and was hired immediately to work as a busboy, which meant going to the agency in the day and then heading to the restaurant at four or five in the evening to start work. I spent my evenings running up and down the staircase of the beautiful duplex restaurant with its massive dining table that had once presumably belonged to Marilyn Monroe.

The restaurant was owned by two brothers and their mom, and they were quite quirky and full of mischief. They were always coming up with different ways to get attention from the press and the public: dressing the staff in wacky outfits, men wearing female attire, the female staff wearing men's clothing and so on. They would photograph us and send the photos to the newspapers on Fleet Street, and the odds were good that a picture showcasing our madness would appear in the press the next day.

But a job is a job, so who's to complain? It was the most fun I'd had since leaving Germany. I was happy to be working both at a modeling agency during the day and making a living at night. Plus, the marketing madness worked. The restaurant had begun attracting some of England's biggest stars, including Samantha Fox and Iggy Pop. I had been promoted to waiter, so I got to serve some of the country's most famous people. Every day was different and exciting.

Then, one Christmas season, the owners decided that they would prop a large Christmas tree against the side of the restaurant's building and seat a fairy on the window ledge above, giving the impression that the 'little fairy' was seated on the treetop like a decorative angel. It was another ploy to get more press and attract more patrons to the restaurant. An English fellow agreed to wear a pink ballerina outfit with a fairy wand and Tina Turner wig and to be strapped to the window ledge with the Christmas tree under his bum. From the street, it appeared as if he was sitting on the top of the tree without support.

The restaurant announced to the press that there was a pink fairy, throwing Christmas crackers and fake snow at passersby, sitting on top of an 18-foot tree in the middle of Leicester Square. It got the restaurant a lot of attention. The press loved the story and covered the fairy smiling on top of the Christmas tree. However, there was trouble in fairyland. One day, the fairy had a fight with the manager about money and quit. This was a disaster. No fairy meant no press and fewer customers.

I guess I had a target on my back that said, "Will humiliate self for money." The owners knew that I needed the money (I was doing more double shifts than anyone else) so they asked me to sit on the tree for the princely sum of five pounds an hour (about eight or nine dollars an hour in the mid-1980s). That was quite a bit of money to make a fool of myself for three to four hours. After I was done, I could still work my regular shift as a busboy or waiter. I would make plenty of badly needed extra cash.

I accepted. I just prayed that no one I knew would see me.

Fairy Tale

So I donned a fairy's pink ballerina outfit, complete with the Tina Turner wig, and sat on that 18-foot tree. I smiled beautifully to all the passersby, throwing them Christmas crackers and wishing them a "Very merry Christmas"! I'm not ashamed of it; you do what you have to do and make the best of things. I did a lovely job, and the public loved it. Sitting on that Christmas tree, smiling brightly and being a "chirpy bird" to lusty, hungry patrons, I started to enjoy laughing at myself. People thought I was funny: they would stop and snap pictures, especially the American tourists, who probably thought that everyone living in England was crazy.

Strangely enough, we started getting more patrons into the restaurant (especially the bar), but even stranger were the fellows who thought I was a pretty "bird" (English slang for girl) and would come in and hang out at the bar, leaving tips and their telephone numbers for me to call.

Imagine their shock when the bartender politely explained to them that I wasn't a "bird" but a "bloke" just like them!

This was hardly my dream job, but I had learned an important lesson: to enjoy whatever I was doing in life. I loved working at Bill Stickers! I loved running up and down the stairs…but in my mind I kept telling myself that one day I was going to make a proper living and that my dream to be a great agent would come true. Trouble was, since I was doing double shifts at the restaurant and I had moved to North London, I was not spending much time at the modeling agency. With Christmas over for another year and my time as a fairy over, reality was setting in again.

One day, Paul, a male model friend from a mixed family in New York, came to London. We had met at Models for Christ in New York years before, sitting across from each other during Bible studies and discussions on the industry and afterwards introducing ourselves. At that time, he explained that he had just come back from Paris to New York and had met someone who convinced him to attend Models for Christ when he arrived in the city, which he did. He told me that he wasn't a model, but his striking crystal blue eyes suggested to me that he could become one. I encouraged him to try modeling, and he went on to become incredibly successful—even appearing in *Elle*, which rarely features male models.

Paul had come to London seeking representation, but after a while he became frustrated and decided to head back to New York. The day he was supposed to leave, I had done a double shift at the restaurant. At about 2:30 in the morning, with the restaurant and bar area quiet,

I decided to ask the manager if I could leave earlier than our usual 4 a.m. closing time. He replied, "If you leave, don't return."

After doing six double shifts within a ten-day period, I was exhausted. I was not going to let a pompous cow give me grief for wanting to leave early. I had not gone to Valerie's agency in a few weeks; I needed the extra money I was making at the restaurant to pay my 40-pounds per-week rent. With the double shifts I was doing, I was bringing in 85 or 90 pounds a week, after taxes. But in the process, I had put aside my ambition to become an agent and was now serving food or bussing tables in a nutty restaurant. Paul was heading back to New York to continue his career in the modeling world; wasn't it time for me to get back to pursuing mine?

I decided it was truly time to "not return." I went upstairs, took off my French uniform, changed into my street clothes, headed downstairs to the bar and ordered a glass of champagne. The bartender knew I was up to something; I never ordered a drink before leaving work. When he asked what was up, I simply replied that I was not returning, so I might as well have my last drink, and a good one. He poured me a glass of the restaurant's most expensive champagne, and I toasted myself.

I had made a fool of myself by sitting on top of a Christmas tree wearing a Tina Turner wig. I had exhausted myself doing ridiculous double shifts on no sleep. Most importantly, I had neglected my opportunity to work as a junior agent at the trendiest modeling agency in London. I thank God for showing me that I had become complacent. I had neglected my dream, and now it was time to return to it. I was pretty sure that God's plan for me did not involve me working as a waiter or busboy forever.

I needed to get back on track and find the island of *Vogue*...and soon. Thank God I had paid my rent that week. I downed that wonderful glass of champagne and, with only 40 pounds to my name, left with my head held high. *Never let them see you sweat*. It was the tagline for an American deodorant brand, and it was brilliant for that moment.

Model Scout

Back at home in Wood Green in North London, I was officially unemployed and broke, with only a few pounds left to my name along with my bible. Abraham was still my inspiration. He had persevered, and so would I.

Even though I had been pulling in double shifts at Bill Stickers, I had kept a relationship going with the area modeling agencies by offering my services to present and place models I knew needed representation. I was now helping models coming from other countries without American or English representation find representation in New York or London. One of my clients was an agency called C'est Bon, owned by a fellow named Bill, who would later play an important part in my career as an agent (and terrify me during the phone calls I've already told you about).

But for now I was playing a different role in the industry: the model scout. I had one foot in the business and the other working in restaurants to pay bills. Then I met Barbara Best, a South African beauty with striking strawberry blonde hair, blue eyes and a baby face that reminded me of a Lolita. This was an era when there were vehement, day-and-night protests against the apartheid government of South Africa outside the South African embassy in London. But despite the potential embarrassment of being from South Africa, Barbara needed an agent. I was going to help her get one.

I introduced her to one of London's top agencies, which eagerly snapped her up. That's how beautiful she was. The agencies loved the women I was bringing to them; I was slowly developing a reputation for having a keen eye. Barbara was bankable and they knew it; so did I.

But on one of her first appointments, I accompanied her to meet one of the world's most famous fashion photographers at that time. His receptionist took one look at Barbara's book and asked her to wait; she wanted to introduce her to the photographer personally. He was shooting Yasmin Le Bon, a supermodel and wife of Simon Le Bon of Duran Duran at the time, but he came out of the studio and said "Hello." Then he opened Barbara's portfolio and, noticing the number of South African magazine covers, blurted out, "Where're you from?"

Poor, calm, sweet Barbara seemed stunned by the hostility of the question. She muttered something that even I could not hear. The photographer asked her again—this time in a stern voice like the one you hear from your angry school principal when you've done something wrong and you know you're busted.

A bit louder, Barbara said, "South Africa."

The man nearly shouted, "Yes, South Africa!" He slammed the portfolio shut, said something I'm not sure of to this day, and walked away. We stood there in shocked silence for a moment, and then we walked away in the other direction. There was nothing for us to say.

I knew then the pain that Barbara felt in not being able to admit where she was from. She knew the pain that black South Africans felt each time they were denied access to their homeland. I was learning a valuable lesson: models are people with their own burdens and troubles and needs. If I was to do my job well in the future, I could never forget that.

Intrusive, Not Obtrusive

Spring had reared its head by this time, and every pale Londoner was scampering to get a bit of color from the sun's rays on a sunny, 70-degree day. The home gardens that are the beauty of London were filled with roses of all shades, surrounded by fields of green. I was reminded of the Sunday school hymn, "All things bright and beautiful, all creatures great and small; all things wise and wonderful, the Lord God made them all."

I was working at a new restaurant by the name of Chicago Meat Packers. The owner was an American living in England who had amassed a large fortune by bringing American-style dining to London. He was a typical fun-loving American in his forties or fifties who made each employee feel respected—unlike the pompous manager at Bill Stickers. Due to his wealth he was part of the elite crowd; each week, different celebrities would pop into the restaurant to have some American-style hamburgers and fries. For example, on opening night I found myself serving the American singer Meatloaf.

Because of this, at our first meeting he taught the wait staff his number-one rule for waiting on important people: "Be intrusive but not obtrusive." Meaning, be approachable and aware of what customers need, but do not get too personal. I would take that success rule with me wherever I went.

While I worked at this restaurant, I continued scouting for models. Then, one day, Tim, a fellow employee who was studying to be a doctor, told me about a program that would pay the airfares of foreign nationals who were willing to work as counselors at summer camps in the U.S. The program lasted for three months—which would allow me to spend the summer in the States and give me an opportunity to reconnect in person with the New York modeling agencies before heading back to England.

I applied and was accepted. I told my boss about the opportunity and, bless him, he told me that when I returned to London, my job would be there. So as summer drew near in London, I was headed back to the U.S., where I would serve as a camp counselor for kids and adults with disabilities. I told my family and my lovely landlady that I would be back in three months time, but that's not how things would work out. The next time I came back to London, it would be on business.

Five

BACK IN NEW YORK

A slew of young counselors boarded the British Airways flight bound for New York. Once we arrived, we were assigned to different states to work at a wide range of camps. I was sent to Maryland to a beautiful little Christian camp called Pecometh, where a bunch of eager young Europeans were tasked with making sure that the young American kids had a great time.

I was determined to make sure my kids had fun as much as the patrons who enjoyed me sitting on a Christmas tree in Leicester Square. But instead of one tree, I found myself surrounded by trees, all set along a beautiful bay filled with canoes. A small outdoor chapel stood facing the water. It was a magical setting. I would sit by the water each evening watching the sunset and give thanks, singing "This land is your land, this land is my land, from California to the New York island..."

Very prophetic.

We spent our days horseback riding, canoeing, swimming and singing Christian songs around bonfires while roasting marshmallows. It seemed like camp for American children must be one of the greatest experiences around. But as soon as we got there, it seemed as if it was time for everyone to leave. As our three months came to a close, all the counselors—American and foreign—gathered together to celebrate the end of camp season with a dinner. During the affair, the other counselors voted me "Most Likely to Make the Best Dad" because of all the fun I'd had with the kids.

I had enjoyed myself so much that I felt sad to leave and head back to London. This was the first time in my life I'd had a lot of time alone to meditate on God's love and the beauty of His creation, especially on the Thursday night chapel meetings with the kids singing songs of praise, teary eyed that the next day they would be heading back home after a wonderful summer at camp. It had been a time of quiet reflection for me without the usual distractions of travel and living in different countries.

My flight to London would depart from New York, but I had about three weeks on my work visa, so I decided to make use of the time. I headed for the offices of New York's top modeling agencies to offer them my services as a model scout in the UK. My first stop was Elite, where I saw an agent friend from London who had moved to New York the year before and was working on Elite's men's board. He asked me what my plans were, and when I told him that I was heading back to England, he scoffed. He told me not to be foolish; there were "better opportunities in New York," he said. I knew that, but since I did not have much time left on my work permit—and since everything I owned was still in my room or at my family's house in England—I had to go back. But the thought of New York wouldn't leave my mind.

Next, I headed over to Bill's agency, C'est Bon, and he asked me what my plans were. I told him about my plans and he said, "Okay, do you want to make some money while you're still here?" Of course, I said yes, and with that I started working with Bill's agency.

Bill liked the way I worked, and the models enjoyed working with me. In fact, I became so caught up in the work that the next few weeks flew by. I missed my flight back to the UK. At this point Bill contacted his attorney, and they secured an extension of my visa and work permit. To make a long story short, I ended up not going back to England at all. Why would I? I was now working for Bill and his sinister Italian-looking friend—working full-time as an agent in New York City! I took the job and moved into my friend Linda's lovely apartment on 103rd Street between Central Park and Manhattan Avenue.

Of course, not everything was perfect in my mind. Elite was *Vogue*; C'est Bon was *Good Housekeeping*. But I was being given a great opportunity to work in New York, so I didn't complain. God was opening doors for me, and the future looked bright, even though the direction of the agency was not the same as I had seen at the top-tier agencies. However, in the long-term I knew that C'est Bon was not for me. Bill was set in his ways; he enjoyed making money from show-rooms and commercial work. If I stayed with him, my *Vogue* dream would remain a dream.

But for the time being, I was content to learn. I stayed with Bill for about a year and worked hard to do a great job—that is, until the day Andrew, a model I represented, and I talked about opening our own agency so that we could represent models that would work with *Vogue*. That was when the threatening phone calls started coming. A few weeks after I ended my confrontation with Bill, it hit me: I was on my own. The Lord had always been my shepherd; now I needed Him to be my agent as well.

The Cowboy

It was time to go fishing for models to represent. Andrew and I had three female models working with us, but one cannot operate an agen-cy with a handful unless their names are Christy Turlington, Naomi Campbell and Cindy Crawford. We needed new faces and we needed to find them.

Then my friend Ken had a bright idea: we would find models by going to New York college campuses at the start of the new semester and scout for fresh faces. I took his advice and posted a flyer on a bulletin board at one of New York's prestigious university campuses. It read: "New model agency seeking models for representation, con-tact…" and then a contact phone number. I didn't know what kind of results to expect, but I got quite a few calls from would-be models.

We met with them, but unfortunately none of them had the *Vogue* look that we were after. Most of the girls were lovely, polite and charming but none looked great enough for us to risk representing them.

I figured that I either needed to scour the city or go fishing in other waters—such as Europe or the Midwest—to find some undiscovered girls who could be transformed into *Vogue*-caliber models. This was not going to be an easy task.

Then it happened! "It" was my final appointment from my college advertisement: a tall, stylish young man with the megawatt smile of an all-American country football jock. He was a real-life, corn-fed cowboy from Wyoming, studying at a university in the city. *Bingo.* I thought I had gone fishing, but instead, I ended up catching a piece of 6'2" prime American beef!

I had the feeling in my gut that I get when I know I'm on to something great. God saved the best for last. Thank you, Lord. This young stud had dollar signs written all over him. I had been fishing for girls to represent, but God knew what I really needed, and He made me a "fisher of men"—or man, in this case. I hadn't been interested in representing men because I had been dreaming of *Vogue*, a women's fashion magazine. But this kid was going to be a star. He may not have been *Vogue*, but he was the epitome of *GQ*: tall and handsome with pearly white teeth.

We chatted for quite a bit, and then I sent him to meet a client. The client called back immediately and confirmed him for a job they were shooting the following week. We had found our first major model and were now representing him along with our small group of girls. Our Wyoming cowboy went on to become one of the agency's first big money makers and is now a major television and movie star.

Dear Lord, I know the model I wanted came in trousers, not a skirt, but I thank you for what you gave me. What I thought I needed was not what you wanted for me. Because of Your wisdom, I did not put all my eggs in one basket by wanting to represent only female models. Because of that, my future would be brighter than I ever thought possible. Amen.

Moving On Up

After this success, we found a few other new models, including the fiancé of a major movie star, and then the agency started to grow rapidly. Before long, we moved out of our cramped office and ended up on the East Side, on 28th Street between Lexington and Third Avenues, in a small townhouse that had a duplex office on the ground floor and two apartments above. This was perfect: we were able to house models coming from out of town during their short working stays in the city.

It wasn't the Ritz-Carlton, but we were happy to have moved on and moved up. We now had two floors to work with. The first floor, with its spiral stairways leading down to the basement, seemed luxurious. Now we had room to run up and down without feeling boxed in. I felt like I was back at Bill Stickers, carrying trays of plates and glasses! But, this time it was models – future supermodels! The Lord had given me an opportunity to "lie down in green pastures" and restore my soul for a time, and I was grateful.

Of course, with growth came change. Andrew was no longer a part of the company and a new financial partner was now on board. Andrew was a true and sincere friend, but I felt forced to separate the business from him as we grew and our financial needs changed. It was the one moment in my life where I had to choose between business and friendship, and I chose business. Andrew and I never spoke again, a fact that I regret to this day. He went back to his assortment of cheeses from around the world while I moved deeper and deeper into the world of fashion.

Things were going well…until one day, disaster struck. Our star cowboy left the agency!

He had decided to go to Hollywood! He was our biggest money earner, and we had booked him for a few national television commercials during the Screen Actors Guild (SAG) strike. The results of those commercials were so successful that shortly afterward we received a call from a charming Hollywood talent agent asking us if we would allow her to represent our models for television and film work. My agency and hers would split the commissions on jobs they booked, since we were not a SAG franchised agency.

I agreed to the deal, but before we could even sign it, they had signed our cowboy to an exclusive deal, cutting us out of any future royalties. Our cowboy was a gentleman; he came to me and my partner and explained that he was going to concentrate on being an actor, which meant that we would not be able to represent him for any print modeling campaigns, at least for the time being. That also meant a major dent in our revenues. Her talent agency would be the only one making any money from his good looks.

That hurt. But I knew there was nothing we could do about it. He was destined for great things, and if I fought to hold onto him he might not have achieved the blessings God had in store for him. He was simply doing what was in his best interest, as all of us do. I was blessed to represent him for the years he was with the agency, but now was the time for him to move on and become something more. So rather than fight, I let him go. I trusted that God had something else in mind.

My lesson from this experience? Do not get attached or hold onto anything or anyone too tightly. God takes us from "glory to glory," and it does not serve Him to have us stuck in one place all our lives. He moves us into different "green pastures." Melissa, one of our agents who loved the Lord, taught me a great lesson in this regard that has stuck with me. Whenever we would lose a campaign or a booking, she would say, "Maybe it was not meant for us. God sees somebody else whose needs are greater at this time, or He has a better deal coming to us."

The thing is, she was always right. God always did have something better coming. So I wished our cowboy well and turned my attention to the crop of potential new stars who needed our time and attention.

Another lesson my team and I had learned by this time was not to force anyone to stay with us, even if it meant losing a lot of money. Some people are in our lives for a reason, while others come for a season. I started telling myself that there would always be other *Vogue* and *GQ* models coming our way; we had to make room for them and to develop a reputation as a place where models could come to grow and to go.

Despite this difficult experience, we knew we were on the right track to discovering models with *Vogue* qualities. We also learned that once on top, they would jump at the best opportunity that came their way no matter how loyal their intentions were in the beginning. It's human nature.

My job, as I was beginning to see, was to make an impact on each of the models we represented—to be a "stepping stone" for whatever else was to come in their lives. I would help them become better models and better people. That would be my mission.

A True Star

While our cowboy was riding off into the sunset, God sent an angel in the form of Mark, an agent from Australia living in San Francisco. Mark was working at another agency, and they had a brilliant model, Andrea Nicholas, whom they thought I should represent. After meeting her, I was delighted to oblige: she was amazingly beautiful, with dazzling eyes that sparkled like diamonds.

Andrea was now the most beautiful model I was representing, and she was equally sweet and patient. She was also the future wife of a major Hollywood star, and in that role she taught me some valuable lessons about representing people who were already famous (or infamous). It seemed that nothing could bother her, even the crush of questions and attention from press when they got wind that she was the beauty that had tamed a huge movie star.

With Andrea on our roster, the press was constantly begging us for information about her. However, we adopted an official "No comment" policy in order to protect her privacy. In all honesty, we had no clue what to say to the media, so it was easier not to comment and move on. We learned not to acknowledge what reporters wanted to hear but to be kind and pleasant by telling them what a wonderful model she was. This became our policy for all our future beauties and celebrities.

One event revealed just how much being beautiful inside trumps appearance, at least for Andrea. She flew into New York to shoot a big spread for one of the hottest magazines in the country. While on the set, the editor revealed something he had conveniently forgotten to tell the agency: they were going to cover Andrea in body paint for one of the shots, while the rest of her body would be naked.

You would expect a diva temper tantrum, right? Not from this woman. She stood patiently and allowed them to paint her body while still being kind and polite to everyone. We only found out about the whole thing after the shoot was over, when Andrea called us to let us know what had happened. She was not even angry! However, we were. The "forgetful" editor got an earful from us.

We were developing a reputation for representing young, hip, edgy, uniquely beautiful models who showed talents beyond just being models. The Lord was providing, just as He had promised.

Six

A-Listers

*A*t the time, Frank Paulson and Amir from A Models were the hottest agents running the hottest modeling agency in Los Angeles. They booked some of the biggest models for *Vogue*, which was a big feat for a West Coast agency. These guys were stars. They had everyone on their roster, and they knew everyone—photographers and celebrities alike. They had invitations to just about every A-list celebrity event—and they were fast becoming an inspiration to me for how to build my agency.

So naturally, one day I went out to L.A. I went to see if I could form some relationships with agencies out there and swap models with them for East Coast/West Coast representation. The reception I got was warm and wonderful. Both Frank and Amir were willing to help and share information about the business—including all the things going on behind the scenes that I wasn't privy to. Frank even introduced me to Herb Ritts—one of the highest-profile fashion photographers at that time, who was shooting every celebrity and supermodel in Hollywood—by getting me an invitation to Herb's birthday party.

Herb had shot Janet Jackson's beautiful black-and-white video with model-turned-actor Djimon Hounsou. When I got my invitation to his party, I finally saw how shallow people can be, especially in a celebrity-obsessed place like Los Angeles. I had told a friend that I was going to Herb's party, and by the end of the day I had calls from people I had never met asking if I could get an extra ticket for them or if they could come with me. To me, it was just another fashion party, but to them it was a place to "be seen."

Olaf, a Swedish model friend, came with me, and he spent the entire evening walking around in awe, staring at all the celebrities at the party. After trying to navigate my way through the crowd inside the house, I decided to go up to the roof to get some fresh air. On my way, I bumped into a beautiful lady in the dimly lit room. She turned around and I apologized for bumping into her. She was so polite and said something like, "It's not a problem. How are you?"

I smiled back and said "Great," while all the models and celebs mingled closely together. She then asked where I was heading, and I told her that I was going upstairs to get some fresh air. She then smiled and said something that I couldn't make out, so I just smiled and said something like "See you later, it's loud in here!" She smiled and walked away.

Olaf quickly pulled me aside and said, "How do you know her? What did she say to you?" I told him that I had apologized to the woman for bumping into her and she had asked how I was and where I was heading. We were just being polite.

He said, "That's Tina Turner!"

Well, God bless her, I'd had no clue! I had wanted so badly to get up the stairs and get some fresh air that I had not paid any attention to her. I should have noticed the hair. But by then I was too embarrassed to go back and let Tina know exactly what I wanted to tell her: that I had sat on a Christmas tree in Leicester Square in London wearing a cheap wig designed to look like her hair. So I said nothing. It was just as well; I had felt like an idiot in a pink tutu, sitting on that silly tree.

Still, this was a party to be at. Thanks to Frank and Amir, I made my debut in Hollywood amongst a crowd of wannabe actors and singers. In the coming years I would make it to Herb's party again, and at one such event in Malibu, a future model of mine named Omar (who later became the James Dean of fashion) and his friend, Tom Blake, introduced me to Madonna. That night, Tom, Omar, Madonna and I had a beautiful time. I knew what Harold Robbins had written about in *The Carpetbaggers*. I was living it!

Street Models

But while I was rubbing elbows with stars in Los Angeles, things were not going as well in New York. Without our star cowboy, and with Andrew gone as a business partner, we had to forge ahead. New stars were coming in, and there were many other *Vogue* models out there ready to be discovered.

By now, we were importing models from Europe. They were beautiful, but at the same time, we knew we were either getting men and women who the top agencies were not interested in, or those who came with, "attachments." For example, we would be promised a great model in exchange for one or two of our new young stars, and then our model would turn out to be someone who did not want to travel or who could only come to New York for one or two weeks, making it difficult for us to present them to clients and get on a plane for a booking.

This is part of the industry most agents detest. I certainly came to detest it. But it is a necessary evil. In order to maintain their relationships with foreign agents, U.S. agents must overlook all these frustrations. The top agencies have leverage because they control access to some of the most in-demand faces in the world.

We did have some incredible American models who were doing well, but agents in Europe were also offering to represent them overseas, which made it difficult to keep them in town working for us. So, we decided to change tactics and "go fishing" in our own backyard, along the Hudson River.

New York City has an eclectic mix of cultures that rivals my native Jamaica. From the Latin American, to the East and West Indian communities, to the Russian neighborhoods, the diversity is exciting and fascinating. So we grabbed our poles, angler's hats in hand,

and went fishing along the Hudson, George Washington, Brooklyn, Manhattan, and Queensboro bridges. And we cast our nets wide!

Thanks to the growth of the company we were finally able to employ a few more agents, including two former models: Maria, from New York, and Chelsea from London. By themselves, they made a great impact on the agency. They worked tirelessly to help build the company even when times were difficult. Then along came Solange, an Austrian former band promoter. With her jet-black hair and shining blue eyes, she was a wonderful character. She lived in the models' apartment upstairs and later on in my railroad apartment on the Lower East Side.

This band of brothers (and sisters) set out to scour the streets of New York before and after work, looking for fresh, distinctive faces who would not be on the radar of other agencies.

We knew that instead of going all the way into the various neighborhoods, we could save time by walking down St. Marks Place, Broadway and all the happening streets where young adults hung out.

That was how we found our Dominican star. He was no more than 5'9", which is impossibly short for a male model. However, in his mind, he was six feet tall. What he lacked in stature he made up for in front of the camera. He was, and still is, one of the most amazing models I have ever seen. His emotions, gestures and attitude made many seasoned models seem like novices. He would do whatever it took to make sure every shot was amazing. The first test photos we saw of him were so incredible that we had a hard time choosing the ones we liked for his portfolio.

He was charismatic with an infectious smile—a natural-born actor in front of a still camera. He was also street smart. He had been in trouble with the law before, so we knew that to keep him out of trouble in the future, we would have to move him into the models' apartment, away from the temptation of the uptown neighborhood where he lived.

He was the first of our "street models" and he opened the flood-gates for our editorial bookings. All the top photographers and maga-zines started calling more often, excited that we were representing these amazing kids with exotic faces. Solange and I were having great fun scouring the streets of New York looking for exotic kids who most of the agencies had overlooked. We were creating our own niche market.

Our street models were even more charming than the norm, not only because of their amazing looks but because of the excitement they brought to the agency. These were not jaded professionals, and the joy of knowing that someone else saw something special in them gave them the motivation to work extra hard to succeed. So even though their commercial appeal might not have been as great as the model types that the magazines were used to working with, they were more motivated to deliver great pictures during each and every photo shoot.

After a few weeks, we realized that we had fallen into an uncon-scious pattern. We were stopping kids with the same traits: most had no idea that they were beautiful, most had gotten in trouble with the law at some point, and most were high school dropouts who were not working. Many were doing illegal activities—such as selling drugs—to survive. To keep them out of trouble, we were now housing a group of them in the top floors of our little townhouse.

Each week, Solange and I would come into the agency from our weekend of trolling the streets bringing in a new exotic-looking kid from Brazil, Puerto Rico, Morocco, or the Dominican Republic—all found on the streets of New York, without taking a flight to Europe, South America, the Caribbean or North Africa. We felt like we were cleverly outsmarting the big agencies, which we were! But this new strategy meant we were also never off-duty. For instance, we might be at dinner and someone with a great look would walk by the restaurant. Our forks would drop to the table, and we'd be chasing them down the streets! Imagine the looks on these kids' faces as we explained that we weren't trying to pick them up—that we thought that they were beautiful and that we wanted to represent them as models.

Most were flattered. Some were quite skeptical. But most would call us.

We knew we were onto something amazing. Not only from a business perspective, but in our ability to give people opportunities that might otherwise never have been afforded to them.

The Lord was my agent and now He was making me His agent for His models. This was a door of opportunity to show others that they were special and could rise up from any situation or circumstances and become successful. Plus, we really enjoyed being around these kids and hearing their stories of life on the streets. Solange became their mother hen and together we kept on fishing.

Harry and Tony

Then, one day, along came Harry. He was the perfect male supermodel. Italian with dark, curly hair and piercing blue eyes, he carried an attaché case everywhere. I'd never seen a male model walk around with anything like that before, but he was serious about this business. For him, going to a shoot was like going to the office, and he was going to make a statement with every client. While it seemed comical, we tried (unsuccessfully) to explain to him that it wasn't hip or cool for a model to go to appointments (usually called "go-sees" or "castings") carrying an attaché case. But he didn't want to hear it.

So when Harry came to stay at our apartment, we prayed that he would not do anything strange. He was a beautiful model with a few loose screws in his head, but at the same time, he was able to get everyone in the house singing a tune: "Big scary Harry ran through the town, upstairs and downstairs in his nightgown..." So he was fun and unpredictable, but we were about to find out *how* unpredictable.

Harry was staying at our apartment on Seventh Street, in the same room as Solange. An influx of new models had made space precious and forced everyone into close quarters. One evening, Harry called

Solange and me into the room, telling us that he needed to show us something. When we went in, he was wearing only his underwear—which he proceeded to pull down to show us the inside of his "teapot" while asking Solange to take a look inside, as he felt there were a number of critters hanging around in his "kettle!"

This was not the type of tea party Solange and I were used to attending, and sweet Solange was not charmed! In fact, she was mortified and furious. In her strong German accent, she shrieked at Harry to "cover the lid to his kettle" and ran out of the room.

Unsure whether to laugh or cry, I calmly took Harry aside and explained that he could not show his teapot to everyone like that—whether he had little friends roaming around it or not. I also sent him to get help to get rid of his "critters." Needless to say, Solange refused to share the room with him that night.

Our life was filled with "characters" and kids with "personality." There was a strategy behind this. For a small agency, finding new agents to work with you when your taste is high and your budget is low can be discouragingly difficult. To get around this problem, we took young, fashionable kids with a gift for gab who wanted to work in the industry and gave them a crash course in booking shoots. In most cases it did not work—most of the kids preferred to hang out in the clubs and party, not get on the phone and sell their souls for models. In most instances, the wannabe agents actually wanted to be models themselves.

Eventually we abandoned that process...but then along came Tony. Tony was my co-worker Chelsea's cousin, which meant she would not take any crap from him, even though they were around the same age. When he arrived in New York from London, we knew we had to have him work with us, even though he was an actor, not an agent. He had no experience as an agent, but his personality was winning enough for us to put him on the phone and hope that he would charm his way into some bookings.

But Tony was an actor, so we knew he was not going to last long. He worked hard at being an agent, but in the end he left to pursue his true passion as an actor and deejay in the music industry. Today, Tony is the man who makes Ellen Degeneres dance as the resident deejay on her daytime talk show, *Ellen.*

Setbacks

For the next couple of years we enjoyed our success: models working with some of the world's greatest photographers and appearing in the world's coolest magazines and some very hip advertising. The trouble was, even having the coolest and most beautiful editorial work—art for fashion magazine stories—didn't always translate to great money jobs, especially for exotic ethnic models, who were not in great demand at that time.

Catalog and advertising work, along with big contract jobs, keep an agency strong.

However, we were sending our top female models who could command those jobs to Europe in the hopes that they would come back to the U.S. with great European editorial portfolios. Unfortunately, it seemed as though as soon as they came back, their European agents would call them back for other work. That meant we were depending on the photographers shooting top fashion editorials for American magazines to bring us their business. That went all right for a while, but then my adopted country went to war in the Middle East. This was followed by a devastating recession.

We had cool, amazing models appearing in magazines both here and abroad, and some big money jobs coming in, but there was never as much money as we would have liked, even in good times. Now, the war and the recession began to hurt us. We were having a hard time paying our bills on time, and the business side of things was becoming a strain on everyone. Our little townhouse no longer felt like our little "green pasture"; the expense of paying the rent and advancing money to models was becoming increasingly difficult to bear.

On top of everything, every couple of months our townhouse was being broken into. We would arrive in the morning to find that our equipment—from phones to fax machines to paper clips—was gone.

Anything they could take, the thieves would take. The police thought that the break-ins might be due to a crack addict who was living in the building behind ours, but I had no clue.

However, setbacks are God's way of telling us it is time to move on. After filing a few police reports and getting no results, I realized that these troubles might be God telling me that it was time to "move with the clouds," close the agency and move on. After the third or fourth break-in, I decided it was time to pack it in.

It was terribly sad. The little townhouse was going to be history, and so were the beautiful kids who had come to depend on us to help them to stay off the streets and give them an opportunity. We had opened the doors by showing them a different world, but now it was up to them to move forward—not look back on their past but press ahead to greater things. Their next move would be their own choice, not mine, and that was as it should be.

On the day the agency was to close I went to a meeting. When I came back, one of our little supermodels and his cousins were packing their vehicle with the air conditioner taken from the upstairs apartments occupied by the models. They were also loading their minivan with some of the agency's furniture! Worse, he and his cousins had kicked holes in the walls leading up to the apartments and written graffiti everywhere.

I don't think he expected me back so soon. When he saw me, he hung his head. We had tried to be a blessing, but in the end, he had taken advantage of us, and we both knew it. I watched him and his cousins continue loading and went upstairs to pack my bags.

We had built something special, but surely it was time to move on. Strangely, I wasn't sad about closing the doors. In fact, I felt liberated and relieved. There was a cloud waiting for me to catch up with it.

Lord, I thank you for our little townhouse. I knew it was not the permanent place that you had intended for me to be. It was a setup for the path that you were leading me on. It was a place of growth, letting go and learning not to hold on to anything.

Part Two

THE BIG TIME

Seven

TRUST IN THE LORD

With the agency closed and no more exotic and beautiful "street models" to manage, I decided it would be best to go and work for another agency. It was the only way to stay in the industry. But I didn't know where to start, so I looked back to the work that had been my greatest success before going to New York: my time as a camp counselor in Maryland.

I had done volunteer work every Saturday morning with a child with multiple sclerosis, helping him to learn and move his body, and I had felt such joy and love going to see him each week. I figured that if I could not work in fashion at this time, I wanted that good feeling again.

Since I was without a job and was used to traveling, I decided that I should try to do some volunteer work with a big international organization.

I contacted the Peace Corps, but they told me that since I was not a naturalized U.S. citizen (I only had a work permit) and lacked an American college degree, they could not allow me in.

I was ready to go anywhere and do anything for anyone: carry water, scrub floors, plant crops, anything to help others. I didn't need a degree for that! It seemed quite silly to me, so I applied to the Young Adult Institute (YAI) and was accepted as a counselor based on my experience, referrals and recommendations. I would work in New York with mentally challenged and physically handicapped people.

I was excited to do this; it came easily to me. However, I was not sure I was making the right decision. Should I stay in the fashion industry? I didn't know, so while waiting to hear from the YAI, I let my fingers do the walking and, once again, opened my big mouth.

I called the top model agencies but not one returned my calls. I knew I didn't need to panic; I had the Lord as my agent. But there were moments of anxiety, especially when one of the hip, new agencies offered me only $18,000 per year to work with them. I didn't know how I would live in New York City on so little money, but I needed to work in my chosen industry. It didn't matter how little I was being paid.

I called back, and I was told to call back again. I called back, and was told to call back again. This went on for a week, until I realized that the owner of the agency was not going to hire me but was afraid to say so. So I prayed. I knew this was a time to trust in the Lord and "be still."

The still, small voice inside me told me to keep trying, so I kept calling agencies. On my final call to one of New York's top boutique agencies, the owner, Carmen, told me to come in for an interview. A former model, she had become an incredibly successful agent and was representing some of the world's most successful models.

This was the bigger opportunity I had been waiting for!

I promised myself that if she gave me an opportunity to work at her agency that I would work very hard to build on what she had created and that she would not regret it. Everything I had learned from building my former agency I would put to use to help someone else. I took the job.

Creating New Stars

The office was in an open, spacious loft with a calm, gentle feel to it. There was an incredible sense of peace and serenity, even with one huge poster on the wall near the entrance that read, "Free South Africa".

Strangely, there were no photos of the agency's star models on the walls; just the poster. That was a powerful political statement, and it added to the intrigue. I wanted to know more about this person who might one day become my boss, who I'll call J. She had the style and grace of a gazelle as she greeted me for my interview, which put me at ease. She was charming, yet strong and commanding, which I liked immediately. She felt like a family member, which made me want to work with her even more. I can't remember what we talked about in the meeting but I left feeling that she was going to be interesting to work with—if I was hired.

What made that prospect even more interesting was the fact that Carmen was representing one of the biggest Caucasian models in the world, a woman from South Africa whose work I had been admiring for years, since the time when she was under contract with Calvin Klein. I could not wait to work with her; she was my favorite model at the time.

In spite of the money, this was looking like a great opportunity. Then I got the news: I was hired! I had already learned to create new stars; now I would be building stars that had already been made. I knew I could not let her down; I had too much to prove.

This job was going to be my "still waters" provided by the Lord. I would lie down beside them and enjoy the restoration, though it would be a lot of hard work! She was a blessing the Lord had put in my life and I was thankful. I called the YAI and declined their kind offer. I figured I didn't need to work with the physically and mentally challenged; I would already be working with fashion models, many of whom suffer from Attention Deficit Disorder. They are used to getting so much attention that they can drain every resource an agent has.

Still, I was eager to start. By being still and not panicking, I was able to weigh the options the Lord gave me and allow Him to help me make the right decision about where to go next.

High Stakes

For the first time in years, I was free from the worry of being an agency owner. My challenge now was to prove that I could perform. For me, wherever I work, it is always hard to think of myself as just an employee, so I worked as if it was my own agency—just in a different location and with more accomplished models that were already tailor-made. I was going to work diligently so that the results would please not only my boss, but the most high Agent who had blessed me with this task.

This was a huge step up for me. Even top magazine and advertising clients were happy to see that I was working with Carmen. Because of her reputation in the industry, doors began to open wider. Even though most of her models had been in the industry for quite a long time, her reputation kept the doors of opportunity open.

I had fun working with women who I had so admired over the years. Now I was being given the chance to build upon what she had already started by keeping her models in the public eye. Of course, at such a high-powered agency the stakes are higher and the workload is much greater, but the rewards of seeing my models appear in the best magazines, campaigns and designer collections made it worth all the stress.

Being an agent really involves two jobs. Apart from representing your current models, you must also add new stars to your roster to replace those who leave the business or can no longer get bookings. I tried to excel at them both. One of the first new models to arrive on the scene was an English rose with ties to the Royal Family. I immediately booked her for a major design house campaign shot by one of *Vogue's* top photographers. Her career was just taking off when, one day, we got news that her father had been killed after being thrown from his horse.

I had never been in a situation like this, but I knew I had to pray not only for her but also for her entire family, asking God to strengthen them during their time of grief. I knew that during this time, she would not be focused on work, so I decided that it would be best to wait until she knew in her heart that she was ready to come back.

During this time, a young English girl walked into the agency carrying a plastic bag and said that she was told to come and see me and that I would be able to represent her. She was not more than 5'7", a little Bohemian, more of an artist type than a model.

Being polite, I asked to see her portfolio. She proceeded to open the plastic bag and withdrew a copy of *Vogue*. She flipped the pages until she came upon the fashion editorial and proceeded to show me a complete series of fashion photos of her—shot by one of *Vogue's* great photographers. She told me that she did not have a portfolio, but there was no need for her to have one; the magazines were her portfolio, and they were stunning.

Wow, I thought. *I just lost one rose and now God has sent another.* We signed her for representation on the spot.

She was the coolest, most unassuming model you could ever imagine, completely unaware of her own beauty and more interested in her passion for comic books, something that was amazing to discuss with her.

I could see that I was now being taken from one level to the next. God was making my work shine by opening doors that might not have opened if I had not been obedient and closed my old agency when I did. If I had tried to hold on to what I had instead of following the clear signs God was sending me, I might have missed out on all of these blessings.

God's gifts kept coming, too. We kept discovering new models, including a beautiful young Filipino model living in Ohio whose exotic look immediately got her on to the pages of *Vogue*. Everything was looking up.

Beautiful People

I spent a couple of years working with Carmen, and our greatest discovery came in the form of a beautiful African-American guy of Jamaican and Chinese descent who later became one of the most successful black male supermodels in the world. Carmen had not set out to represent male models, but when he came into the agency, it was clear there was no way we would let him leave the building without signing him to a contract.

We got him an advertising shoot for Ralph Lauren and when the photos for the campaign came out in the magazines, the designer received congratulations for taking a chance on using a dark-skinned, unknown model in such a prominent campaign. All the coat jackets that our model wore in the campaign sold out immediately. Lauren shot him again soon after, and that campaign also proved successful.

We also had a beautiful Caucasian guy, who we had signed right before this African-American model, and he had taken off as well, shooting some of the most beautiful covers of the top men's magazines in the world. Now we had our salt and pepper, ebony and ivory. These two guys were amazing: diverse, yet similar in that they were both recommended by people who thought we should represent them even before they became models. Today, the beautiful African-American model is not only one of the world's biggest supermodels, but also a television star. So we clearly were doing something right.

We also had an incredible mixed-race Asian model, a young woman who had become a star before I got to the agency. She became the youngest model ever to close the Chanel show in Paris for designer Karl Lagerfeld—at the age of 13. Today, she too is a huge television star and a designer with a multi-million-dollar clothing empire.

One of my most amazing finds came when I was at a summer concert at Tompkins Square Park: Wigstock, a concert filled with people dressed up in wigs, male and female. As an agent, you never know where you will find your next star model, and this was no exception. I was surprised to see an incredibly beautiful guy with movie star looks standing nearby with a lady, possibly his girlfriend or wife, and a friend. I wanted to go over and give him my business card but was hesitant. As evening started to fall, I realized how tired I was. I decided I had to be courageous and talk to the young man or walk away and miss an incredible potential opportunity.

I walked over to the lady he was with and told her that I was a modeling agent, and said that I would like to speak to her about representing him. It turned out he had just arrived in New York a few days earlier from his native Barbados and was actually a model who had worked in Paris before and had decided to try New York! Can you believe my good fortune?

It's amazing how God works. I hadn't wanted to even go to the concert that day, but being bored, I decided to go anyway. I had wanted to go home without speaking to the young man, but something made me change my mind. Sometimes God will lay something on our hearts to see if we will be obedient, even if it means going somewhere we do not want to go or doing something we do not want to do. He places people in our paths in places we would never dream or expect.

The young man told me he had just arrived in the city and was going to visit modeling agencies the following week. I invited him to come to my agency before he went to any others. Now, I had a new challenge: to convince my boss to take him on as a client. But to my surprise, she was not interested in our agency representing him at all! But I knew in my heart he was going to be a star.

To avoid my boss' anger, I hid his pictures in my desk and sent them to a group of top photographers and clients to get their reaction. Before the week was over, the calls started coming: the clients all wanted to use him for the campaigns. Immediately, I booked him for the new Versace campaign shooting in Miami with one of the world's greatest fashion photographers, Bruce Weber. He had three jobs confirmed before I had the courage to go to my boss and ask her permission to take him on as a client!

When I finally did so, she was wise enough to say, "Yes."

I felt proud. I had felt in my heart from the start that this young man would be extraordinary, and I was right. It was not a feeling of gloating but a feeling of excitement—I was as happy and proud as a parent with a child who had received accolades. Then other campaigns started flooding in for this new star, from Calvin Klein to

Guess Jeans. He was later named one of the top models of the year and was featured in the *New York Post*, the *New York Daily News*, and on countless television programs.

We had another star.

Biding My Time

But while everything was going great, I started feeling that it might be time to move on. I had been with Carmen for about four years, and I was working much harder and longer to help the models succeed. But I was also having a hard time paying my bills. I was also receiving offers from other agencies; the agency that had not taken my calls when I was willing to work for only $18,000 now said it was willing to pay me $80,000 per year, twice my current $40,000 salary. It was temping, but Carmen had been the only agent who took a chance with me when I was down and without a job. I knew I could not walk out on her now, not when everything was going great. I knew I had to bide my time and see what God had in store.

The year before, I had told my boss that I was looking to leave the agency because I was unable to pay my bills. She promised me changes, along with the possibility of one day being a partner in the company. Well, some changes did happen (the addition of one additional agent on the booking board), but I didn't see much of a change in my paycheck. My loyalty was making me late in paying my bills. Expenses are very high in New York, and I was also helping to take care of my family, which, on my salary, made it impossible to keep up with my bills.

I faced a decision: stay and hope that my boss would give me a part of the business, or move on and take my chances with another agency. Then I found out that most agents in my position were making between $150,000 and $300,000 a year! That was a huge disparity. I had also been promised a bonus, which I would receive on a certain date. As that day approached, I wrote some checks totaling the amount that had been promised, but on the day I was supposed to receive the bonus, there was nothing. The accountant informed me that she was never told of such an arrangement. I knew it was finally time to move on.

I told my boss that I was leaving the agency and that I would give her three weeks' notice. I had stayed because of her willingness to take a chance with me when no one else wanted. For that I'll be eternally grateful, but at the same time I knew that I could only be thankful for so long. I also knew only God could repay her for the kindness and blessings she had bestowed upon me. I had tried to do the right thing by being righteous, but in doing so I was deceiving myself, believing everything I was told while knowing that I could not pay my bills. It was time to make a change.

I had to find a way to cover all the checks I'd written based on the promise of the bonus money (which never came in) before they started bouncing. So, at the end of the following day, I headed straight to another agency that had been calling me for months. The agents there thought I was joking when I walked in and said I was going to be working with them starting on Monday.

And that's the way I made my switch!

Dear Lord, you "restore my soul" especially when I'm obedient to your will. I had learned to step out in faith in closing my agency, and become a blessing in building someone else's company, all while trusting you to approach a stranger to represent even though my boss said no to him. I was obedient and it paid off. Thank You!

Eight

THE MAKING OF THE SHREW

*M*onday morning came and I was working for a different agency. It felt strange, but good: being in a new place and knowing that the full burden would not be on my shoulders alone.

Interestingly enough, I had no idea how much I was going to be paid when I started, nor did I ask. It didn't matter to me; I just knew it had to be better. I also knew that God would provide.

Well, my starting salary was $80,000, double what I had left. Now I was being paid fairly; my job was to make sure that my work reflected my pay. A few of the models I had discovered at Carmen's agency followed me to this new agency, and that helped. The owner of the agency was a charming, business savvy woman with an air of grace and sophistication that was beautiful to see. After being a successful agent in South Florida, she had opened a branch in New York, seeking to duplicate her success in New York. She was willing to get some of the best agents in the city to help make her dream come true.

I was eager to prove that I could do something great for her. For the most part, the agents worked together like a family. There was (and is) a lot of insecurity and rivalry in the fashion industry, which can be quite destructive. There were some instances of it here, but for the most part we were a team working toward the same goal.

Because I was working on the women's board handling the female models, I also did double-duty handling the young man from Barbados whom I had found at the Wigstock concert.

I didn't place him on the men's booking board but represented him through the women's division. This was a strategic decision: far more calls come in for female models than for male ones. When I fielded these calls, this gave me a chance to ask the client if they were interested in any men. It was common for clients to call one agency for their female models and another for their males, often overlooking the other division within each agency. This gave me an advantage: I could present the young man for work before the client could make another call.

Sometimes this trick worked; sometimes it didn't. But before too long, he was working a full schedule as busy as that of any of the girls on the board. In fact, at times, his chart had more confirmed jobs than some of the top women. He was also one of the top five money earners for the entire agency.

Contracts

I forged ahead. I was now blessed to work with one of the smartest agents in the industry, who I will call G. He was given the responsibility of handling the top editorial clients while I was given the task of bringing in the big-money advertising campaigns. I missed dealing with editorial clients, and from time to time I would find myself battling with the other agents to be allowed to book editorial work—especially when the clients would call and actually ask for me.

But I also loved the notion of bringing in big bucks for the company.

My success not only meant more *Vogue*-level work, but more time dealing with contracts. Most agents hate reading or writing contracts, because it can be tedious work, especially if you are not a lawyer. But this was one of the best parts of the industry for me. I loved contracts. I treated them like I was a detective: instead of simply signing what clients gave to me, I would comb through each word, sentence, paragraph, and then cross out, delete and amend the content as needed. I was reading business and entertainment books and articles about contract negotiations, and following the careers of top entertainment agents, including sports agent Leigh Steinberg (the inspiration for the movie *Jerry Maguire*) and Hollywood super-agent Michael Ovitz. I learned from their negotiating tactics and brought them to my work negotiating deals for my models.

Some clients did not like to be dictated to. Others did not like amendments to their contracts. The way I saw it, if they wanted a model, we would need to compromise so that each party would be satisfied. So I did not back down. On one occasion, my knowledge of contracts really saved us. One of our partner agencies in London had decided that they were going to pull one of our top models from us and place her with one of the biggest agencies in the industry because she was now taking off and shooting *Vogue*. G. had done a wonderful job developing this beautiful, 5'7" English blonde girl and had pushed and sweated to get her in with the top photographers. Now that her labor was coming to fruition, our "partners" were going to snatch her away!

I was in the middle of negotiating a contract for a cosmetic campaign shoot at the time involving this model who was about to jump ship. Sensing that she might leave our agency at any moment, I sent a brief note of agreement to the cosmetic client stating that if the job was suspended until a later date then the deal would continue to be negotiated with our agency once it was revived. Anytime you are dealing with contracts, anything can go wrong. Clients may change their minds, their concept, shoot dates and any number of other things. So I knew I had to lock this client up.

They signed the agreement, and I held on to it until the day came when the agency in London decided that the English model was going to switch to the other agency, which was also in New York. As is customary in the industry, I sent the list of jobs pending for her, along with the shoot dates, to her new agency in New York. I made sure they signed an agreement to comply with the various possible shoot date options, as well as future pending contract negotiations.

Months later, after the model had switched agencies, we got a call from the client with whom I had been negotiating the terms of the cosmetic campaign shoot. They had finally settled on their shoot dates and were set to resume the negotiations. Once the deal was completed with the monies agreed upon, I then contacted the model's new agency to let them know of the new shoot dates. They were surprised but agreed to comply with the shoot dates once I produced the agreement that both they and the client had signed months earlier, which gave me the right to book her for this campaign.

But her agents in London were furious. By having both the client and the other agency sign agreements to work with my agency, I had ensured that the work would go through us, giving us the commissions and all future bookings pertaining to that campaign. Basically, by using contracts as a strategic tool, I had prevented the London agency from completely pulling the rug out from under us. Of course, they did not like this one bit. They refused to give us any dates for the model to shoot with the client and demanded that the deal go through them and them alone.

Not so fast, I replied. *We have a deal signed by the client and her agent in New York.* I told them that our agency would sue them if they did not comply with the contracts. We won that round.

It pays to know what's going on in other industries in entertainment. I'm surprised to this day how many agents still don't take the time to study the business side of fashion, especially how to negotiate and read contracts.

The "Shrew"

Then there are instances when you have to agree with your client no matter how much it hurts, especially in the wallet. One of our models had been booked for a one-day catalog shoot in California and had agreed to do the job for $15,000. But on the day of the shoot, she did not turn up. She was in London, and she had decided she did not want to get on a plane to get to California.

This put us in a difficult spot. If she had told us that she did not want to do the job, then we would not have booked her for it. But the minute she agreed to do it, she would be held responsible. We took the ethical road and agreed with the client: she had to pay back all the money she would have made from the shoot, as well as all the expenses related to the production of the shoot, which had been scheduled and set up at a cost of thousands of dollars.

She did not want to pay the money, but we threatened to terminate her contract if she didn't. In the end, we were able to give the client back the $15,000. It was an expensive lesson, but it also established us as an agency that did the right thing—something that is rare in any business.

During these days at this agency, we faced many wonderful challenges and had incredible bookings. We would celebrate our good fortunes on Thursday evenings. We knew that Friday was coming, and it was a way of celebrating the fruits of our hard work that week. Our offices were on West Broadway in the SoHo district, in a beautiful triplex loft space. It was magnificent to walk in and go upstairs to our booking room or to the third floor, which led to the rooftop deck. We were usually too busy to go to the roof, but it was lovely to know it was there.

The agency had grown to be quite big, and we were enjoying great success. Our male model from Barbados was still doing great and was still being booked on the women's board, making him the envy of the other male models within the agency. I had been nicknamed "The Shrew" by the other agents because I was shrewd in my negotiations, my bookings and in the rates I would demand for my models—even unknown ones. I was not afraid to ask for what I thought was fair, especially when it came to contracts...and I would fight for what I felt was right.

For example, right after starting to work at the new agency I was told that no one else was making any more than I was. It was okay for someone to make the same salary as I made, but not more. I liked the idea, so I had the agency put that clause in my contract. Well, after about a year working there I asked for a statement from the accounting department in Miami regarding some of the models that had followed me from Carmen's agency. But when the statements came, the envelope also contained a salary sheet of all the employees and agents. This clearly showed that another agent was making well over $100,000 per year—a violation of my contract.

I was shocked and surprised. My employer had signed the contract stating that no one else would make more than I was. The next day I called my boss in Miami and explained what I had just learned. She denied that anyone else was making more than I was, until I told her that I had the salary statement that her own office had sent and the name of the person who was making more.

I wasn't trying to be a bully. I was just trying to be fair. We had an agreement, and I had more than lived up to my part of it. I only wanted them to do the same. God has a strange way of revealing if someone is taking advantage of us.

I demanded a new contract. My bosses and I met in Miami, and over a meal they offered me the same salary as the other agent was making. I rejected that deal. I knew that I was the "money agent" in the company, bringing in the majority of the company's income. How could they justify paying me the same as another agent whose billings did not add up to anything close to what I was earning? I knew what I was worth. God had shown me that He could raise me up on wings of eagles, and I did not intend to back down.

Finally, they gave in. I signed a new contract that paid me far more money than the other agent with additional bonuses and benefits given as an incentive to keep bringing in the top contracts. This meant dollars and *sense* to everyone. I was not going to let what happened at my previous agency happen again. I was going to fight for what was right.

I was also called "The Shrew" because I did not like losing a booking or having mistakes on a job, especially if they could be avoided with a phone call. But on the whole, I would let mistakes slide. I tried to remind myself that everything happens for a reason, which it always does. But I think my reputation for shrewdness was set in stone when one of my most successful models got pregnant. I was negotiating a cosmetic contract for her, but the dates kept changing. By the time the contract was finalized, she was six months pregnant. My beautiful Eastern European model with sharp blue eyes, jet-black hair, and cheekbones chiseled like a sculpture, was going to have a baby. She was overjoyed about it—but this was going to be a big contract, and she did not want to lose it. Neither did I.

She was going to shoot a series of commercials and photo shoots for about ten days in California. Normally, I would have told the client about her pregnancy, but this was an opportunity that I did not want my model to lose. The only way to find out if we were going to have to let the client know about her pregnancy and cancel the job was to get a copy of the storyboard. This would give me an idea of what the photographer and art director had in mind. So I asked. Hopefully, she would not be wearing a bathing suit.

Talk about divine intervention! When the storyboard came, it had her wearing large sweaters and coats. They wanted the shot to reflect fall and winter. My model was showing, but she was not yet as big as she would have been at nine months. She went to California for the shoot, and the clients never figured it out. On the second or third day of the shoot the stylist did, but, bless her lovely little heart, she kept her mouth shut until after the shoot. In the end, the client was happy and my beautiful model received a large payday and a handsome contract.

Ignoring Rivals

I was constantly striving to be successful, and for that reason I did not want to know what other rival agents were doing. I would see their star models in the magazines, advertising campaigns, on TV shows and on shoots with my models, but I saw no need to be friends with them, even though I had a lot of respect and admiration for them. I knew I had to keep blinders on. I would get annoyed if another agent mentioned what other models were doing; I would usually change the subject. I didn't want to worry about what others were doing; I wanted to keep my attention on doing the best for my models. I would think, *Why are they looking at what the others are doing, when they should be fighting for their people?* It didn't make sense to me then.

It was an exciting time in fashion. The diversity of models was growing, and fashion was in a state of euphoria. I loved Naomi, Christy, Cindy, Linda and all the other supermodels. I would get excited to see what their agents were doing for them, and I swore that even if I never made it to that level, I would at least try to get close. John Casablanca from Elite Models and Paul Rowland at Women models were the two agents I most admired in the industry, along with Ivan from IMG. They were intelligent, creative, superb agents who really cared about their models.

By watching what these giants did, I learned and put those lessons into action. I was becoming even more fearless in the prices I was asking for my models. Some of these prices did not make sense—some of the models had little experience in the industry—but I knew their earning potential and was eager to start them at a high price.

Others were already stars, so it made sense to fight for a high day rate. One model had been in and out of the business but was still quite famous, especially once when she and her celebrity spouse turned down more than a million dollars per year to endorse a skin care campaign for another agency. Her husband had advised her not to take the deal, which in retrospect might not have been wise, as she never received such an offer again.

Another one of my top clients only wanted to photograph a model's back, which meant that no one would know who she was. That did not matter to me; if they needed to shoot her that badly then they would have to pay. And pay they did! For a one-day shoot on which they could have shot anyone in the business, they ended up paying

$90,000 plus a $25,000 bonus for some extra shots. Carré Otis, the on-again, off-again girlfriend/wife of Mickey Rourke, walked away with a princely sum for having her back photographed. No one ever saw her face.

But the most ridiculous thing was when models allowed boyfriends, girlfriends or drugs to cloud their vision so that they made stupid mistakes. Such was the case when one of my male supermodels based in Paris started turning down jobs because he and his agent were high on heroin or cocaine. I had met him years before at my tiny agency when I was representing his fiancé, a beautiful German model. He became one of the biggest models in the industry, and years later we were still friends. One day he told me that he was going to switch agencies and wanted me to represent him; I was only too happy to oblige.

But it is hard to mix business with friendship. You're often unable to say the things you want to when your friend starts making serious mistakes. My male model friend had become incredibly famous, especially in Europe. When we walked on the streets of Paris together, it was amazing how many people would shout his name or stop to say hello. When we went to his agency, you would see girls lined up outside and on the stairs waiting to see if he was there. He was a rock star. But to me he was still the young, beautiful, innocent kid that first came to New York with his girlfriend, and it broke my heart to see that he was now under the influence of his European agents who were snorting and shooting up drugs with him.

His drug habit was out of control, and no matter how much we tried talking to him, it seemed to fall on deaf ears. His agent in Europe was one of the best in the industry but also a man with a serious drug problem, which made some of his decisions appear totally irrational.

For example, we had negotiated a non-exclusive deal to shoot a clothing line campaign for a top design company for a day rate of $190,000, along with a catalog shoot for one day at $30,000. We were all set for the model to fly in from Paris to New York for the shoot— when his agent abruptly cancelled the shoot!

This addicted agent demanded that we cancel the shoot or, better yet, go back to the client and demand more money. It was absolutely absurd. I was not about to do such a thing; the agent and I had conferred during the entire negotiation and had both agreed that the shoot was a great deal for everyone. The deal died. It was the most ridiculous example of how drugs can destroy a model's career. Years later, with all his money gone, spent on drugs, the model ended up in rehab, broke. Still, we remained friends and are friends to this day.

Dear Lord, what may seem like valleys or dire situations in fact always turn out to be my greatest blessings. I know that in order for me to become stronger in life I have to pass through some valleys, but it is the way I will handle the journey that will determine how far I will go in making it to the mountaintop.

Nine

MADONNA AND THE "CON OF CAHN"

ow that I was working with top models, I was also hanging out with a much more interesting, accomplished crowd, including a man named Jacob Cahn. One cool summer night, Jacob and I were heading up Ninth Avenue towards Central Park, having a great laugh after leaving a brilliant fashion bash in Midtown. Now we were going to attend a Democratic Party fundraiser for then-President Bill Clinton. With us were four young Latino men who were working on their first music single. Jacob was their manager.

We were all laughing as we walked instead of taking a taxi; it was a beautiful night, and we were in no rush. After a few blocks we noticed a car driving slowly beside us; we had not taken much notice of what was going on in the street—that is, until the car stopped and a beautiful lady got out, flanked by two or three of what must have been bodyguards.

Jacob said something, indicating he knew who she was, but I was caught up in a conversation with one of the singers I had represented when he was a model by the name of Miguel. All of a sudden, the four young, beautiful Latin guys started grinning. I suddenly noticed that the woman was wearing a pair of jeans that hung low, showing what looked like a pair of men's boxer shorts. As she walked up to us, she smiled.

I said, "You're quite sexy wearing men's boxers." She smiled back, and then turned to me and said, "Whatever you do, don't trust him. Don't trust Jacob *Con*." All the guys started laughing. So did I; their laughter was so infectious and vibrant that I couldn't help myself. Now they started ribbing Jacob and calling him "Jacob Con."

Jacob was furious, of course. He did not like the way she was having a laugh and walking with us, ignoring him even when he tried to discuss two of her chief dancers that he represented. She ignored him and started to talk to us about where we were heading. We told her about the party and invited her, but she declined, except to let us know that she lived not far from where the party was happening.

Madonna (yes, that's who she was) walked with us until we got to Central Park and 59th street, and then she bid us adieu. I didn't remind her that we had met years before at Herb Ritts' birthday party, but she wouldn't have remembered me anyway. She was still as beautiful as I remembered her from that party, and she's still beautiful today.

As for Jacob, Madonna's semi-prophecy sadly came true. He went from being a manager to becoming the biggest fashion stylist in the entertainment industry, working with all the big-name singers. But years later, he was arrested and jailed for fraud. Allegedly, he had borrowed expensive jewelry for some of his celebrity clients for photo and video shoots and lavish premieres and never returned the jewels. It was a sad end to a promising career.

The Future Kennedy

As the success of our agency grew greater, we brought in some new directors to help us grow in new directions. However, many were mean, miserable people who had been in the business for a long time and had become bitter and disillusioned. They became *detractors* who did more harm than good. One was a female hardliner who, in one second, could be sweet as apple pie and the next as sour as lemons. I stayed out of her way as much as I could and focused on what I was paid to do.

By now my salary had increased because of the amount of money I was bringing into the company. I had a Dutch model who had done amazing work in Europe and had moved to New York; she was making quite a lot of money doing terrific editorial work and catalogs but had not done *Vogue*. I had introduced her to Calvin Klein, and she became one of his favorite models, doing 'looks' and 'fittings' and typically making $7,500 for each eight-hour day, plus overtime. She would sometimes work every day for two or three weeks and make a lot of money.

Then, one week prior to New York's famous "fashion week", while this Dutch model was working, I came back from lunch to find the bitter female director yelling a slew of profanities at me, telling me that I had "sold out" the model for less than what other models were getting. This was nonsense; I had been told by Carolyn Bessette—the future Mrs. John Kennedy, Jr., who was working at Calvin Klein at the time—that no one would be making more money than our girl unless she was an even bigger name. So, after being chewed out with the kind of foul language you might expect to hear from a sailor, I went to my desk, dialed Carolyn's number and had a chat with her.

I had been doing business with Carolyn for years, and she had always been honest and direct. We had a great working relationship, and I trusted her because of her honesty. While working at the former agency on North Moore Street, I would occasionally see JFK, Jr., who lived only a few doors down. Each time I saw him, he would always acknowledge me with a nod or a hello.

Now, he was marrying a client that I had been doing business with for years. I'd always had a great time working with Carolyn, and she was in love and quite happy.

I asked her if there were any other models doing the same kind of work as my Dutch girl and making more money. She said yes. The model was a top *Vogue* cover girl, and she was getting a day rate of $9,000. Also, this model was only doing one day's work, not weeks of consistent work like our girl was. I thanked Carolyn for the information, went back to the board and calmly told the foul-mouthed director what Carolyn had said. Embarrassed, she said nothing.

A few days later, I got a call from Carolyn. Apparently, she had seen the angry director on the street and tried to speak with her because she and Carolyn had worked together in the past. However, the director was unprepared for the unladylike words Carolyn unleashed on her in defense of me.

Now I was being defended by a future Kennedy. I had hit the big time! It seemed that every step of the way, God was putting great and important people in my space to warn and defend me.

TWA Flight 800

One incident that I'll eternally be grateful to God for happened in 1996. I had to walk away from a booking that I wanted because my model was not able to travel to Paris. This ended up saving her life.

We were working with a beautiful young blonde model with a short, pixie hairstyle that was new to the industry. I was excited to work with her as she had an air of fresh, clean-scrubbed beauty that was "All American" and very different from the grunge look that was hot at that time. The year before there had been a lot of controversial press given to the Calvin Klein "CK" campaign due to its raw sexual images and the way that some of the models in them had been portrayed as being underage. President Bill Clinton had even condemned the images, which starred a number of our models, and others had called the campaign "kiddie porn." One ad in particular showed our English rose, lying on her side with her legs parted, and this caused outcry from parents around the country.

We were part of a controversy over the age of the models in the campaign, which was frustrating because all our models in the campaign were over 18 years of age. While I understood why some people had been offended, the fact is that when a model does a shoot, there may be images that cause controversy afterwards. Calvin Klein definitely knew how to push buttons and generate a fortune in free publicity!

In this environment, Tracy, our young "All American" beauty, was a refreshing change. She was starting to enjoy her success when we signed an option for her to shoot a fashion story in Paris with one of my favorite photographers, Rico Puhlman. I had always admired his work and was excited to have her travel to Paris to shoot the job for an Italian magazine named *Amica*.

Well, I always believe that God has His hands on my life, my work and the people I work with. Tracy was quite special to me; I loved her enthusiasm for the business. It was always lovely to see her walk into the agency to greet everyone with a big smile. She was scheduled to leave with her crew for Paris at the beginning of the week and work with the other models who were going to be in Paris at that time.

As it turned out, God had other plans.

Hunt Richter, a client in Canada, was doing a catalog shoot, and I had suggested Tracy for it. Because of the booking schedule, I thought she could do both jobs. If I set things up just right she would be able to shoot the catalog in Canada and then travel to Paris to shoot the magazine. Rather than flying over with the crew, she would travel a day later, and she would miss the first day of the three-day Paris shoot.

Well, the Italian magazine was not happy about this—rightly so, as I had given them the "first option" to use Tracy as one of the models on their shoot. But I was adamant. I felt that she could do both jobs, and I confirmed her for the catalog shoot in Canada. I was not about to have her lose a good-paying job even though I wanted her to do the editorial work as well. I knew she needed the money. High-profile editorial work gets models into the bigger design houses, fashion shows and ad campaigns, so it is important even though it does not pay well. For the catalog, she would be paid several thousand dollars—a lot for a young model starting out and trying to pay for rent, clothing and all the other expenses that come with being a model.

We tried to make it work so that she could leave Canada early and travel straight from the airport to Paris with the crew. But the client wasn't buying it and released her from the shoot in Paris. I was hurt, but also happy. Tracy was going to have money in her pocket. She went to Canada, did the catalog shoot and traveled back to New York. As Amy headed home, I went home to relax for the evening. Just as I turned the television on, there was a news flash: a TWA jet had crashed after taking off in New York. It was the flight that Tracy would have been on, traveling to Paris with the photography crew. Everyone on board TWA flight 800 died, including the photographer, Rico.

My heart sank. I stood in front of the television, stunned.

When I was able to think about it, I realized that while I had tried every way to get Tracy on that flight, God had intervened. He had a reason and a plan for her, but I had been blind to His warnings that the Paris shoot was not meant for her. I had nearly cost her her life. So while I cried for the passengers and crew, I also cried tears of gratitude to God that He had spared someone that I cared about. If Tracy had died that day, I'm not sure if I would have stayed in the industry.

Sometimes, we never know why the Lord put obstacles in our way, but I truly believe the Lord was protecting the models I worked with. Looking back, I realized that each day I would pray for God to protect our models as they walked the streets of New York, London, Milan, Paris—wherever they had to go to work. But I hadn't realized until that moment that God had heard my prayers and had kept watch over them. Because of His love for me and the people I worked with, I believe Tracy was spared from such a tragedy. The Lord was truly my agent!

Love Letters to God

Now, I was starting to write daily love letters to the Lord in my notebook. Before taking phone calls from clients, I might write a note to the Lord that said, "Dear Lord, thank you for this day! Thank you for the models you've given us to represent. Continually guide and protect them everywhere they go and grant them favors according to your will. Bless our clients and bless the agents as they too work to do your will! Amen!"

They were short, simple prayers that became daily reminders of God's blessings. I was growing closer to the Lord and wanted to make sure that I honored Him in every way possible.

One of the blessings I believe the Lord has given me was the gift of compassion and encouragement. I put this gift to good use when I noticed that one of the models we represented had a drinking problem.

She was one of the sweetest models anyone could ever meet. She always came to work with joy and love for others in her heart. She had been a nomad born in Somalia, but she had become a successful model working with every major fashion magazine and designer. At that time, she was a Revlon spokesmodel.

One day, she opened up to me by sharing some of the things she had gone through in her life. The story broke my heart. As a young girl, she told me, she'd had a dream that one day she would get out of Somalia. Her mother held her down, screaming, while an old woman with a rusty razor blade cut her clitoris. This disgusting genital mutilation was a tradition in her culture, a way of ensuring that for women, sex would not be seen as pleasurable but only as a form of reproduction. Female Genital Mutilation, or FGM, is still performed on young girls all over the world and has been condemned by the United Nations.

When my lovely model was only 13 years old, she was offered in marriage to a man in his sixties for the price of a few head of livestock. Even in the midst of life as a nomad, she believed that there must be other things in the world. One day, she left her family and traveled by foot through the desert, even staring down a lion, and made her way to the capital of Somalia, Mogadishu.

Her story was one of great bravery, faith and hope. In Mogadishu, she found family members who told her that one of her uncles was going to London and he was looking for a maid to look after his kids there. She begged the uncle to take her with him, and unwillingly, he did. After a few years in London, her uncle told her that he would be returning to Somalia and that she would have to accompany him. Determined to stay, she buried her passport, forcing him to leave her in England.

Then one day, while she was working at a London McDonald's, a photographer by the name of Donovan Mitchell (at the time, one of the official photographers of the Queen of England) stopped her on the street and gave her his card, telling her that she was beautiful and that she should call him as he would like to photograph her.

Understandably, she dismissed him as a pervert and did not call him. However, she kept his card and decided one day to check to see if he was legitimate. She figured that she had nothing to lose. He immediately booked her for one of the world's most prestigious fashion calendars, put out by the Italian tire company, Pirelli. She worked with top supermodels like Naomi Campbell!

Almost overnight, this former nomad girl became one of the worlds most sought-after fashion models, gracing the pages of *Vogue*. She told me that she had not dreamed of becoming a model, but I knew that God had other plans for her than just being a nomad girl married off for a few camels. God had taken her from the sands of Somalia to the pages of *Vogue*.

However, for years she had dealt with the pain of the circumcision and the crude methods used to sew up her vagina, which made it uncomfortable for her to use the bathroom and caused her great pain during her monthly menstrual cycle. This led her to drink alcohol as a way to ease the pain. Also, the hurt of not knowing where her family was also left her depressed. Nomadic families move from place to place, so there was no way to send them mail or phone them to find out if they were all right.

After she shared her life story with me, I knew in my heart—as a friend and not just as an agent—that I had to do something to help her. I knew that she needed to share her story with others so that she could help other young girls who were at risk of suffering from the barbaric practice of genital mutilation. I wanted her to use her life as a blessing—to move beyond the pages of *Vogue* and speak out.

I went to the director of the agency about her story and was told that no one would be interested in it. I was undeterred. My contract would be up in a few months, and I wanted to be more of a manager than an agent. I had approached my boss in the hopes that this would be one of the first projects I could tackle. I calmly told my boss that if she did not help me with this project by allowing me to work on it, I would leave when my contract was up. This was too important an issue to ignore. God had placed it before me, and I was not going to let it disappear.

I truly did not want to leave the agency; I was really enjoying the work, but I knew I would leave if it meant that I had to commit to this cause.

To keep from losing me, my boss gave in. She would help me tell the model's story to the world. This reflected the view that I had developed: that as agents or managers, we were there to help our models with their lives, not just their work. If there was something serious happening, we as agents needed to step up to the plate and help in as many ways as possible. I knew I needed to help this brave young woman get her message out and overcome her addiction.

Before long, *Marie Claire* magazine ran a story depicting her plight. We then started moving to get her a book deal. I felt the only way to get the story out to the masses was through the media, but it was too long a story to be told in a magazine article. We met with two literary agencies and both wanted to represent her for a book deal. We chose

Christy Fletcher of the Carol Mann Agency because of her passion for the project.

In the end, this young model got her book deal! But after the deal was signed, my contract negotiations with the model agency stalled. One month before expiration date, we still had no new deal. I was out of patience: I told them that I would be leaving the agency after my contract's term ran out. I think they thought I was bluffing; when the last day of my contract (a Friday) rolled around, I went around to the other agents, kissed them and finally got a chance to use the exit line that "Mad Amanda" had taught me years earlier. I said, "I love you all, but I've got to go!" And I was out the door.

The last comment I heard from one of the agents was, "He's being silly. He'll be back on Monday." My boss called on the weekend, but the deal she presented was nothing more than what I was getting at the moment. I told her that I would not return and that I was going to be focused on doing more humanitarian work.

On Monday, I did not go back. Six months later, the agency closed. One of the agents who was very close with my boss went to the agency on a Saturday morning, took all the contact files and all the model portfolios, and took them to a rival agency. So it goes in "the business."

For my part, after leaving the agency I went to work getting my model's story out. One of my first stops was the United Nations. They had read her story in *Marie Claire* and were only too happy to have a face that would lend a voice to their push to stop the practice of FGM around the world. UN officials named her a special United Nations Goodwill Ambassador for Women's Rights, focusing on FGM. It was very exciting.

By now, her book promotion was going well, including an exclusive interview with Barbara Walters for ABC's *20/20* program, which brought even more attention to the issue of FGM. She was also named one of *Glamour* magazine's top ten women of the year, was featured in *Vogue* with fellow supermodel Iman as part of a photo shoot by

Annie Leibovitz, and was a special guest at the Amnesty International awards along with stars like Richard Gere, Muhammad Ali and Julia Roberts.

I was so proud of her success. She has made a huge impact on lawmakers by speaking out and sharing her story. As a result, laws have changed all over the world, banning Female Genital Mutilation. God had used her adversity to help others. He had given her the covers of magazines, but the most important gift He gave her was the will to tell her story, a gift that changed or saved the lives of many young girls and women around the world.

Today, this beautiful model is still making a difference around the world, sharing her story and saving lives by being a blessing. Not bad for someone who just wanted to escape being a wife traded for a few animals!

Lord, you are always with me, even when my dreams are not as clear as I would want them to be. You have given us all a dream to do something special through the pain and heartaches of our lives. You help us shine brightly in whatever tasks are given to us. This was by far the best job I ever worked on as an agent—and I didn't earn a cent from it. Amen!

Ten

THE PLAGUE

*N*ot long after helping my beautiful model become a UN Goodwill Ambassador for Women's Rights, my good friend Ken met the winner of the 1998 Miss Universe pageant, Wendy Fitzwilliam, from Trinidad & Tobago. Her reign as Miss Universe was coming to an end, and he thought I would be the right person to represent her, since she would need management for all her post-reign endorsements and appearances. We met and, perhaps in part because of our shared heritage, decided that we would work together.

I was focused on helping others now, and I knew that with Wendy's name and former position, I could help her to do a great deal of good. She had an organization in her native country called The Hibiscus Foundation. It was for homeless children with HIV/AIDS who had been abandoned by their parents or whose parents had died of the disease. She had gotten doctors from America to travel to Trinidad to treat and monitor the drug treatment for the kids so that they could live beautiful, productive lives.

I knew that the UN would be happy to have such a popular public figure to help bring awareness to the plights of children and women with AIDS in the Caribbean and other regions of the world. The UN embraced Wendy and also gave her a position as a United Nations Goodwill Ambassador (UNFPA) on the issues of children's rights around the world. This was thrilling!

Then one day, Wendy told me that the Red Cross in the Caribbean had contacted her because they were having problems on one of the islands. People had shown hostility to having a home for adults with AIDS in their neighborhood, especially on one of the islands, so the hospice had to keep moving from place to place. Each time they settled in a new region, someone found out what they were doing, and they would have to pack up and move again. It was stressful and terribly expensive. This was sad news to me, because one of God's teachings is to "love thy neighbor as thyself."

The AIDS plague had become very personal for me. I had a good friend from Jamaica by the name of Fletcher, one of the most talented designers and tailors I had ever met, with a sense of humor that was infectious. He had worked with my superstar cowboy when he arrived in New York. We had not seen each other in many years, though he had called me about a year earlier to tell me that he hoped that we could hang out one day, have a good cup of tea, and laugh about how far we had come in life. We had always joked that one day we would go back to Jamaica and produce a fantastic fashion show.

Little did I know that Fletcher was quite sick. He had contracted the AIDS virus and had stayed away from his friends and family because he felt ashamed and thought that they might ostracize him. We had agreed to meet one Saturday to go to the movies, but I ended up traveling and failed to call him to let him know. But as usual, Fletch (as everyone called him) forgave me and told me that he needed to share something with me. This was just his personality; he would chuckle and tell silly stories even when we would talk about serious issues, so I didn't think much about this. I told him we would talk in a week or two. But I never heard back from him.

Two or three weeks later, I received a call from some mutual friends. Fletcher had died. My heart was sad; he had been one of my best friends. I did not know that he had been sick, much less infected with the AIDS virus. He had been reaching out to tell me something, and I had not reached back to listen. My focus on my models had caused me to neglect the friendships I had grown up with. Fletcher knew that I would not judge or condemn him if he had shared the news of his disease with me, but I think the stigma of being Jamaican and having AIDS had hurt him deeply; he feared going back home to die.

My friends told me that Fletcher had become unable to work and at times did not have enough money to afford a meal. This broke my heart even further. I was making quite a bit of money at that time, and I would have gladly shared it with my friend if I had known about his situation. Fletcher had been one of the most joyful, stylish, impeccably dressed gentlemen I knew; he would never go outside without dressing up. Every event he attended was a cause to celebrate his style. From him, I learned a great deal about the fashion industry.

Betrayal

For every step in life that we take there are many hands outstretched to help us on our journey. Fletcher's hands helped guide me and shaped my steps to this day. In order to honor him and the children Wendy was working with who had AIDS, I decided to start an event in the Caribbean that would help build more hospices for children with HIV/AIDS. It would be a fashion event that would take place once a year, similar to fashion week in New York, Paris, Milan, and London. Caribbean designers and heads of government would be involved, and the event would be on a different island each year. Most of the proceeds would go to help build hospices on islands that were suffering most from the AIDS epidemic.

I knew this would be something I could do, not only knowing that I could honor a friend on a grand scale, but also knowing the good that would come out of it. That made me even more excited to get it done. I knew I needed a partner in the Caribbean, and the only person I could think of was in Jamaica. Fortunately, he had invited me to Jamaica to judge one of his model pageants. I went, and the next day over breakfast I told him that I would like to partner with him to produce the yearly event. He loved the idea and told me that he would love to be involved! I explained that I would be able to bring the press and people I knew in the fashion industry, creating a lot of attention.

I also told him that Wendy, the former Miss Universe, could be the honorary chairperson. He told me he was excited to share this dream with me.

As I left the island that day, I was ready to work on this project, fulfilling not only one dream but the dreams of many. Unfortunately, it did not happen that way. A few months later, a friend informed me that the event was going to happen—but without me onboard! She explained that the producer I thought I had a deal with had approached her. But instead of asking her to be involved, he had asked her to produce the shows, cutting me out of the project that I had conceived and brought to him.

Henceforth, the opportunity to help build hospices for children who were HIV-positive or who had AIDS—to help the Red Cross and fulfill the wish of my friend Fletcher—would happen, but not according to the original vision. Today, the event is a successful international showcase that takes place on the same island where I envisioned it would, but it is an event largely designed to increase people's personal wealth and prestige. It has nothing to do with sharing.

One can only imagine how many Caribbean kids and adults infected with HIV or with AIDS would have benefited from the funds raised by these events if they had been done as originally intended: for the sole purpose of giving and helping, instead of producing a profit. It was a lost opportunity to bring hope to those without hope.

Not long after discovering that the event had been snatched away, the UN press office contacted me with a great opportunity. Would I help convince other Miss Universe winners to become UN Goodwill Ambassadors for the United Nations Population Fund (UNFPA), attaching them to issues related to children and women's rights around the globe? I was delighted. This was an incredible chance for me to do something I enjoyed doing: linking people together and making a difference.

I engaged Wendy's help and got the names and information of women she thought would best serve the people and the issues. In the end, five former Miss Universe winners from Asia, Europe and elsewhere were selected as Ambassadors, raising awareness about issues related to women's and children's rights in their regions. This culminated in the Miss Universe winners being chosen to be part of the UN Goodwill Ambassadorships program, helping spread awareness of women and children's rights issues in developing countries.

New Opportunities

My former Somali model was now getting lots of press and invitations to speak. She had signed her book deal, but I was not getting any of the commissions. So I had little money left in my pocket to sustain me.

With my finances depleted, a friend from Austria called me one day to find out if I would be interested in meeting with a gentleman who had an agency in Los Angeles. He had opened another office in New York and was having trouble getting top editorial bookings, even with the top agents he had hired.

There was unease in my heart over this. Something told me that I should not go back into the business, but looking at my finances I decided to meet with this entrepreneur. By the end of our meeting, I had a deal to manage his New York office. I would sign a two-year contract, which would give me carte blanche to manage the agency as I saw fit. I would be paid handsomely, with a lovely six-figure salary. I also would still be able to manage my Somali girl and all my personal projects, especially those with the UN.

But I knew I could not do this on my own. I needed God's favor to guide my eyes, hands, feet and mouth toward the right models and the important people in fashion who could present those models with work. I also needed a team of agents who would understand my vision and be willing to work with it to make us all successful.

One such person was a beautiful French agent named Claire who had been working with the agency but was not sure what role she should be playing. I saw in her the ability to be great, so I decided that she and I should partner together and build the image of the company's New York division. It was a great decision. Claire proved to be one of the best agents I had ever worked with: smart, charming and a hard worker. Most importantly, she was a great listener.

After engaging Claire, I told the other agents which clients I wanted them to focus on. I was very clear; I wanted there to be no excuses for things not to go as smoothly as they should. Then I set out to fix the problems in the agency. One of the first things I noticed was that all the models had just about the same style and look: they all seemed to be from California, cute but not with the international flair of the models I was used to working with. I knew that this was not what New York was looking for.

So I cleaned house by dropping 90 percent of the models being represented. I kept the dozen that I thought would be needed to help pay the bills until we got better models to build the agency's image. My philosophy was simple: I would rather have one great model to work with than 100 second-rate models

After that, I was off to Paris.

Eleven

UNCONVENTIONAL WISDOM

*P*aris is one of my favorite cities in the world. With its incredible architecture, great cuisine and amazing art scene and museums, it is always a joy to be there. Also, because of the work I had done there with many models—and because of the work I had done on the model who became a special UN Ambassador —I was given the choice of some incredible European models to represent at the New York agency.

The Parisian agencies wanted their models to be marketed in a certain way, and I was only too willing to comply. Amelie, a beautiful friend who was also an agent, showed me some of her girls, and instinctively I knew the ones that I wanted to represent. They were all incredibly different, quirky and quite unique. I knew most of the top agencies would not have chosen these girls because they were not conventional beauties, but I knew they were the kind of models that I would enjoy working with.

I was also getting a reputation for representing unconventional-looking models, which suited me fine. Some of the girls were strange to look at, but I knew that they would fit perfectly with my style of booking. I was not sure if my boss would enjoy having these girls at his agency, but since he had given me carte blanche to revamp the agency as I saw fit, I was going to take a risk and do something the other agencies were not doing. To me, that could be a disaster or a formula for success.

I went back to New York and presented the first girl who I thought would bring recognition to the agency. She was a Scandinavian beauty with the feel of a Modigliani type model from a different century: long, flowing red hair, a small face and doe eyes that made her look like a canvas ready to be painted. I knew she could be a star, but I also knew that the only photographer who would understand her look— one who I trusted the most and who had always been an incredible support of my models—was one of *Vogue's* biggest stars. I wasn't sure they would be interested in such an unconventional beauty, but upon seeing her portfolio they requested a meeting with her. We had her flown in, and immediately she was booked to shoot Italian *Vogue*.

When the magazine came out three months later, not only did our model have about 30 pages in the issue, but she was also on the cover! The cover of *Vogue*! The agency had its first *Vogue* cover, and it was with the beautiful, quirky model that the other agencies had ignored and passed over. This was perfect. It was the breakthrough we needed. God had once again blessed my hands in selecting models that I knew I would enjoy working with. I had accomplished what I had promised. They wanted *Vogue*, and I gave it to them. I was being paid to deliver, and deliver I did, with God's help.

One Success After Another

After this success, my team and I began showing the photographers and magazines a different type of beauty each month. All the agents did their best, and it was evident in the way the agency grew. One after the other, we started to have more girls doing *Vogue* and other top magazines, which was quite exciting.

At this point I knew the blessings had surely come from above and that God had answered my prayers. I had prayed for His divine hands to bless my work, the agency, the models, my co-workers and every single client that would call the agency. He had surely answered my prayers, and now I was going to glorify Him in the industry in a very special way.

I had gone to a restaurant called Lola's in the Chelsea neighborhood of New York and found that they held a gospel brunch on Sunday mornings. I knew that many people did not like to go to church, so I thought *Why not take them somewhere where they would be fed physically and spiritually?* The gospel brunch seemed like the perfect way to entertain my models and to glorify the Lord.

So on that first Sunday, at the start of New York Fashion Week, all of my models went up to Lola's and had a blessed time singing songs of praise with the choir! Everyone in the restaurant, including our models, enjoyed themselves. It was a small way of giving glory to God and getting the message of His love out through music. The choir was amazing!

Because most of our models were Europeans or from countries where gospel music wasn't performed, many had always wanted to see a gospel choir. They were blown away by the gift of seeing one in concert. Later, some started coming to church with me because they were touched by the music and the love that was displayed.

After that promising beginning, we had a blessed season with designers, producers and casting directors. We then started creating unique promotional materials that would get designers excited about our agency. We did not want to send the usual "model cards" to designers; we wanted to get their attention by doing something different. Once, we made circular cards of our models and put them in CD packaging. This got the designers thinking they were getting a box of compact discs, only to find the images of the models when they opened the box.

Each season, we would come up with something different, which made sense, as our agency had built a reputation for being innovative. This kind of creativity helped to set us apart. As a result, more *Vogue* shoots were coming our way. It seemed that we had at least three models in every issue of Italian *Vogue*, as well as all the other major magazines. Our doe-eyed redhead had set a standard for the rest of the models to follow, and we made sure that they were of the same caliber as she was.

From Russia With Love

Then came one of our biggest discoveries, by way of Russia: Candide. She had a long, pencil-thin figure and would stride like a gazelle on the catwalk. She would become one of my favorite models of all time, but she was no ordinary model.

Candide stood out because she was intelligent, smart, classy and incredibly fashionable. This was no ordinary supermodel in the making; this was someone with the ability to either become a major star or walk away from the industry at the peak of her career. She knew that with her brains and style she could do whatever she wanted. I had to tread carefully with her, but at the same time, there was something special about her that had me in awe.

I was not the only one enamored by her; the photographer who had put my Scandinavian model on the map was also smitten with her. In a short time, the demand for Candide was so great that she was fast becoming the darling of the top Parisian designers and editors. But eventually, the day came when I had to bring her to America. I had to handle her U.S. debut with care, or I would lose her.

I had started negotiating an exclusive deal with one of America's most famous and controversial designers. We had completed the first part of the contract that would introduce Candide to the press and the public by having her both open and close his show—something that only the top supermodels in the industry have ever done. But the most interesting part of the deal was that she would be replacing one of the most famous supermodels of all time, someone who had been under contract with the designer for ten years before the designer decided not to renew her deal.

I knew this was going to set the industry on fire, so I made sure to say nothing to anyone about what was going on. Candide and I had developed a wonderful sense of trust, because each time we had a chance to do a shoot and she did not want to do it, I would not force her to. I respected her feelings and let her pick her own opportunities.

Unfortunately, my boss, excited by what was about to happen and knowing that his agency would have the model who would replace an icon, decided that he would contact the press to let them know that our model would be the new face for this designer. Before I knew what was happening, one of the newspapers broke the news the day before the show. I got a call from the designer's representative, lashing out at me for leaking the information to the press. Although it had been my boss' name and the agency name in the newspaper, I got the wrath of the client. They had been negotiating with me, and to them, I was responsible.

As an agent, I was never interested in divulging information to the press, especially about those models that were in relationships with celebrities or those who became celebrities themselves; it was the same with any negotiations. It was part of my job to protect their privacy, and that meant not sharing anything personal or business related about them. It was important for me to stay in the background, out of the spotlight, and help them achieve their dreams. I was the agent, not the talent.

As you might guess, after my boss decided to hog the spotlight for the agency, the deal fell apart. We had only signed the first part of the contract, which allowed Candide to open and close the show. The client was so angry about the press leakage that the second part of the deal, which would have had her photographed for the campaign and bring in major dollars, was abandoned.

Still, Candide's debut on the New York Fashion Week stage was amazing! I stood in the audience as looks of awe and shock appeared on the faces of many of the press in attendance. Everyone was saying, "Who is she?" and "Where is so-and-so," the supermodel who normally opened and closed all of this designer's shows. Our Russian beauty made a lot of headlines, including the front page of the *New York Post*.

The press went crazy over Candide and put more labels on her than you would find in a designer showroom: anorexic, razor thin, skinny, and more, forgetting that the former supermodel she had replaced was of the same body type but just shorter. Not all the press was mean-spirited, however; many embraced the change and were quite smitten, not only with her beauty but also with her smarts. I was amazed at how calm and poised Candide was during this period of intense scrutiny.

Even though the rest of the deal had been ruined by the press leak, our lovely Russian had created a media storm upon her American arrival. This only made her appeal to other clients even stronger.

Eating Disorders

Our Russian winning streak continued with another model of Russian descent that we were just starting to represent at that time. Like Candide, she had the flair of a ballerina, with short blonde hair that we loved. She had a lithe, elegant body with features that were reminiscent of a 1940s-era model such as Dovima, one of the most famous models of all time. She was in private school, so we had to be careful to work shoots around her classes.

However, there were times that I noticed that she looked a bit too thin. I decided to have a talk with her to make sure that she was eating properly and not being foolish. She assured us that she was eating well. I remained concerned. Because of the pressure to stay thin, eating disorders are common among models. I had seen a similar situation with a model from Canada that I represented back when I had my own agency. She lived with me for a while and kept insisting that she was healthy, but the only thing we ever saw her eat were chickpeas. If she ever had a salad or anything else, she would go straight to the toilet. It became clear that she was bulimic, a dangerous situation.

She ended up moving to Europe and spending more time there, until one day her agent called me from London to discuss her eating problems. They, too, had noticed what I had pointed out. They were concerned also and were thinking of sending her back home. In the end, she ended up moving back to Canada—and away from the industry—to regain her health.

Now I was in a similar situation with my young Russian, who was playing Russian roulette with her health. No doubt she was a *Vogue* model in the making; I knew that she needed to meet with the same photographer that had made my other girls successful. But I was cautious.

In my heart, I felt that something was not right, but after she insisted to us that she was healthy, I sent her to meet him.

As expected, he loved her and booked her for a *Vogue* shoot that would take place on location in New York instead of in his studio. However, a few days into their shoot, I received a call from one of the associates working on the set: they were concerned that she was not eating. This confirmed my suspicions. I had not listened to that still voice warning me about her health problems, and now others were seeing them also. This was not the way for anyone to be exposed—especially since news travels like wildfire in the world of fashion.

Fortunately, I knew the photographer and his crew were good people who cared about models. That's why they called to warn us. I spoke with the model and asked her to eat, telling her that everyone was concerned about her health. If she could not take care of herself, I told her, she might never work with this photographer again. I also told her that after the shoot we were going to have a serious talk about her health.

She assured me that she was okay and that she would eat. But on the third day of the shoot, she collapsed under the bright lights. Apparently she had not eaten anything at all that morning, and the heat of the lights was too much for her. We agreed that she should not finish the shoot, so I had them send her home. Her dreams of *Vogue* were over, for now.

I was grateful for the sincerity with which the photographer and his crew handled everything. However, my main concern was for the model. I knew we needed to get her some help, but she had to start by being honest with her situation. Plus, she was not yet 18 years old, so while we could give referrals for doctors, everything else had to start with her parents.

I called her mother and delicately explained what had happened and why we could not represent her until they sought help for her. We could resume representation at a later date once her health had improved, but for the moment it was better for her not to be put in a situation where she would feel forced to look perfect. This is a part of the industry that always made me sad: young models so desperate to succeed that they will do anything—even destroying their bodies—to look perfect for the clients, designers, stylists and photographers.

In the end, some of the photos that my Russian beauty did before falling apart actually appeared in *Vogue*, but her career never became what it could have been.

Forgiveness

Addiction and eating disorders are big problems in entertainment and fashion. That's why I generally did not like working with models under the age of 16. There is just too much pressure to look and stay perfect. Because being rich and famous have become so important, a lot of parents will sacrifice their child for their own selfish gain by saying things like, "The kid wants to do this." But in an industry that is based on physical appearance, it is tempting to try "shortcuts" that can cause them real harm. Models are often quite insecure and spend a lot of time comparing themselves with each other.

I once represented a *Vogue* cover model that was in her early twenties but had become quite famous at the age of twelve when she made the cover of one of the major fashion magazines. Now, she had three major problems: drug addiction, weight issues and debt.

Even though she had been earning more than a million dollars a year by the age of 16, she was broke. Her addiction consumed all of her money, and now she had started stealing.

It was heartbreaking. This was one of the sweetest models I've ever worked with, and by the time I was representing her, she had all this baggage. Some of the top agents were refusing to represent her because they did not want to have to handle all her problems. Others had already represented her and were distancing themselves from her due to her drug problems and theft allegations.

Forgiveness can allow a person to heal, but in our industry forgiveness is only applied to those who are still bringing in millions of dollars. Agents will cover and overlook drug habits, bad behavior or other problems a person brings to the table as long as the cash is still coming in. But if there is no money, forget about it! I have a hard time understanding why parents allow their kids to enter an industry that can treat someone as the most precious commodity in the world—until that person is down. At that point, the person is disposable. It plays on the psyche of models to know that they are dispensable. I believe that is what causes some models to turn to drugs, while others desperately seek love with boyfriends who turn out to be parasites.

I did not want that to happen to this model. I chose to represent her not because of her potential earnings but because of the hope that in some small way, I could make a difference in her life. It is hard to see someone down and not try to help. I thought that perhaps God had placed her in my path for this reason. She had many demons chasing her, and yet I knew I could be the friend that could help guide her in the right direction. She had the potential to be bankable again, but at the moment it was not possible. Still, that did not deter me from wanting to represent her.

It wasn't about the money; it was about the impact that one person can make on someone else's life. This was about letting her know that someone cared about her even as she was at the end of a dark road and people were turning their backs to her. If she chose to leave the industry, I wanted her to do it on her terms, with dignity and compassion—not feeling patronized. I was going to treat her with the same respect as the other models, including those that were on top and the ones new to the industry.

Lost Cause

I was even more concerned about her daughter. She had the most amazing child by a previous boyfriend who had taken all her money by acting as her manager, and taking cash advances from clients against future earnings, and then abandoning her. Other than stage parents, boyfriends are the worst, especially those who work in the club industry in New York, Milan and Paris. They manipulate models into making stupid mistakes because they know that models will listen to them more than their agents or parents.

Many careers in our industry have been destroyed because girls listened to boyfriends playing upon their insecurities. No matter how we tried to explain to a model what could happen and to be careful, often she would listen first to her boyfriend, regardless of how manipulative he was. My addict former star model had done so, and her beau had left her with debt, his child, and nothing else.

As it was, the model's weight was a major problem, so I decided to get an honest opinion from a photographer I trusted—the photographer who had made her a major star. After seeing her, he told me how beautiful she looked but wanted her to lose around ten pounds in order to shoot her again. With someone else this would not have been an issue, but with her it was going to be difficult. She had a new boyfriend who many suspected might be a drug dealer.

After representing her for a while, things got worse. We started having a hard time contacting her for bookings or appointments. But I knew we could not give up on her.

She had an amazing, touching relationship with her daughter, and for that reason we decided to make one last effort to save her. She was an amazing model with a beautiful heart who was always trying to please others, but the demons in her life kept her from moving forward.

She agreed that it would be best for her to leave the business for a while, move back to California to be near her parents and seek treatment there. That's what she did. Sadly, later on she made headlines in a different way: "Supermodel Arrested for Identity Theft." But God is great, and today she has turned her life around and has become a beautiful mom with three incredible kids, living a blessed life.

Dear Lord, I will follow and listen to that still voice you place in my heart, even if I'm not sure about my own decisions. Help me to make the right decisions and continue to follow your clouds.

Twelve

SPIDERS AND SNAKES

The Vogue shoots kept coming, along with all the other major fashion magazines and campaigns. With them came attention and respect from my peers in the other agencies—but also a lot of envy within the agency I was running.

Toward the end of the first year of my two-year contract, changes started to happen on our booking board. Additions were made to the staff that seemed great but were actually quite troubling. Again, I had the feeling that things were not quite right.

My boss explained that the changes were made to help us grow. This made sense (even though, to me, no job or client is too small), and I was thankful to have additional agents on board to help. I thought this would give me more time to focus on the major clients who were now calling the agency on a regular basis with requests for our models.

It was around this time I learned a great deal about the "spiders and snakes" in our midst. First, one new agent came. Then another. Slowly, the mood in our vibrant, joyful, tranquil agency changed. Staff meetings were filled with shouting and obscenities, generally directed at me. Usually the rants and screaming were about my influence over the top clients; this infuriated the new agents.

I explained that this was the nature of the business. Clients always prefer to speak with the agents they have a relationship with, and I had developed trusting relationships with them. I also pointed out that there were other clients who preferred not to speak with me and had relationships with other agents, and that did not bother me as long as we took the calls and booked our models for their shoots. That was a blessing to everyone, I said.

It finally came out that one of the new agents hired to handle the catalog and advertising clients was actually the new director of the agency. My boss had not said anything to me, but that did not matter; my job was to deliver *Vogue* and all the great advertising campaigns. Title and position did not interest me. My main concerns were my models and ensuring that I was paid fairly for my work.

But things got bad. Two other agents, Cathy and Victoria, and I would go to the toilet every morning to pray before starting our day at work because we never knew what was going to happen. I would also pray at home before getting to the agency, and I would close my eyes and say a little prayer during these meetings or excuse myself, go to the toilet and pray for God to give me strength to make it through the days, weeks and months until my contract expired.

Things became even more comical when one of the agents— who was always screaming in the meetings—asked to join us when he found out we were praying each morning. I was not sure if he was sincere, but in any case, we obliged.

It didn't matter to us. We were happy to include him and let God work His will. I felt like I was in a battle that I had brought on myself when I took the deal to run that office. God had warned me not to take the job, but because of my stubbornness I did not walk away. In my heart I felt that the Lord was giving me another opportunity to leave the place again.

Bitten

During these crazy times, the work kept coming in—and with it came offers from other top agencies asking me to switch agencies. I had the option to walk away at the end of my contract, but my boss told me that he was going to renew it. I did not want to renew my contract, knowing the situation at the agency. But I told myself that I could do another year. Surely, it would go by quickly. It's amazing how we deceive ourselves.

About one month before the expiration of my contract was due, around September 1, I felt that something wasn't right. I had not received any new contract to sign. At the beginning of August, I contacted my boss to check on the status of my contract. Was it going to be renewed? If not, I was going to meet with other agencies. Three times I called, and each time I got the same answer: "Yes, of course we are going to renew it. Why would we not, after all you've done for us?"

A promise is a comfort to a fool. I was sure being made one.

Onward to beautiful Brazil for my annual vacation, but when it was over I hurried back to the agency to prepare for the show season. I could not leave the models stranded without proper preparation. Well, I guess being in Brazil had affected me. I came back to New York with a "Que sera, sera" mindset.

However, I did meet with the president of one of the top agencies who had asked me to listen to their offer to change agencies. At Starbucks, we hid in the back and they made their offer. I explained to them that my boss was renewing my contract and that I was reluctant to renege on my promise. They explained to me that they felt that my contract was not going to be renewed and that I should think about it and call them in a few days.

I knew I should have said yes to them on the spot and accepted their deal. But I kept my big mouth shut and declined their offer. It was a stupid move. But in my heart, I feared that all agencies were the same: just more egos to deal with.

I knew that I was afraid of letting someone down. I also knew that I had to leave because I was not being treated right, but it took me a year to do so. I felt guilty at the thought of hurting someone or their business, even if they were not doing right by me. Later, I started learning to let go and let God do His will—to not be a pleaser of people. After all, we're all in God's hands.

But this time, I turned down the offer, went back to my same old desk with the same snakes and kept dodging them while chasing the same dreams of *Vogue*. Then the snake bit me.

I was bitten by my boss, and it happened so fast that I hardly realized it.

On the day my contract expired, my boss told me he would like to have lunch with me to discuss some commissions due to me. I was so immersed in preparing for the upcoming shows I had forgotten about my contract. We went to lunch at a lovely Italian restaurant on West Broadway called Il Tre Merli. But we did not get very far into our lunch before my boss dropped the bomb.

"We will not be renewing your contract. You have to leave the agency today."

My fork came down.

Is this a bad joke? I thought.

It wasn't. The message had been clear for a long while, but I had ignored it. I must have said something or looked at him at a certain way, because he said something like, "Yes, today. I want to thank you for all your hard work and all that you brought to the agency." I was so stunned that I can't remember the exact words.

I had been blindsided. I was also angry because the meal was good and I could not enjoy it. At least he could have waited until after the dessert before dropping such vulgar news, or told me at the agency, after lunch.

I thought of my meeting a few weeks earlier with the president of the top rival agency and how I had blown a great opportunity because I had trusted someone who had now stabbed me in the back. What a coward! He could have been honest with me when I asked if my contract was going to be renewed or told me the night before so that I did not come into the agency that day. But instead, he had to ruin a good meal.

Now my cow of a boss explained to me that the two agents who had orchestrated my ouster would love for me to become their publicist! If not, I would need to get back to the office and collect my belongings, as a new agent was arriving shortly to take over my desk. Well, I knew that was not part of God's plan for me, so I thanked him for the offer and gently declined it.

I had become too comfortable with the snakes around me and assumed I would not be bitten. Not only did I lose the deal from the other top agency, now I was out of a job. I was being pushed *far* outside of my comfort zone.

I tried to blame my boss for what happened, but there was no one to blame but myself. God had opened a door of opportunity for me with another agency that was far stronger than the one I was with, yet I found so many reasons not to walk away from the snake pit I knew. I was afraid to walk into my land of milk and honey.

By the time I got back to the agency, everyone knew I was a goner. You could hear a pin drop as I walked in. But I walked in with my head held high, took my bag and walked out. "Onward Christian soldier," I sang to myself!

My friend Cathy was a great comfort to talk with during this period. With a few gentle words, she explained that God wanted me out of that place because my time was up. Even though I knew this, it was a wonderful confirmation to hear it from someone else who I trusted. I was able to let go of the hurt and move on. I was over feeling sorry for myself.

I knew that this was just another lesson in life—and that there would be many more to come. As long as I was prepared to allow the Lord to go before me every step of the way, I had faith that I would see His will and my own dreams fulfilled.

Ironically, one of the two agents who plotted my ouster was given the same royal treatment about six months later when the agent who had hired him decided to get rid of him because he had become too powerful.

Resurrection

There's no doubt about the goodness of God. He makes us shine even when others try to shame us. He takes us from "glory to glory", and I was a witness to this. I knew that the best way to walk away from a bad situation was to leave with my head held high, even if I was pushed out on my backside. As I left the agency, I still had one final *Vogue* cover, which came from a model that had been in the business for years and was successful during the 'heroin chic' period of fashion.

A few months before my sudden exit, I was in Paris. An agent from one of the top French agencies I worked with asked me to meet with a model who had not worked in America for years. She thought I could do something miraculous to revive her career. I think they offered her to me because no one else was interested in representing her; she was considered "out of fashion" and old, even though she was still in her twenties. That is a sad commentary on the industry.

Anyway, I have always loved a challenge, so I met with the model at my hotel in Paris. Immediately, we hit it off. It was as if two old friends had been reunited; we chatted for a few hours about her work, her husband in Italy, how the business can be cruel, and her past work in New York. I felt in my heart that I needed to represent her. It was a special task, and I was up to the challenge. God would help me to bring new life to her career.

I took some Polaroids of her, took them back to New York and sent them to the photographer who had shot her for *Vogue* in the past, telling him how beautiful I thought she looked and that he needed to see her again after so many years. I believed he would see something special in her as I did…and it worked!

I had her fly in from Milan to meet with the photographer in New York. No longer was she sporting the "heroin chic" look; now she was a mature, beautiful woman, ready for her second chance at *Vogue*. Her dreams came true—again she was photographed for Italian *Vogue*. Not only did she make the pages of the magazine but the cover!

God had used me to help resurrect a model's career by positioning her with the right people who would help her write her second act. I was able to leave my old job knowing that I had accomplished what God had intended me to do. Now, He had other work for me to do, and I was ready to go wherever He led me.

How to Build a Supermodel

A few years earlier, I had turned down a request from a top French agency that wanted me to work in their New York office. However, the new president of this agency knew that I had done a lot of work trading models between New York and Los Angeles, and he called after hearing how the serpents had booted me out of my previous job and made me an offer: would I be willing to come and work with him, immediately?

I had received offers from some agencies in the city, but I felt peace in my heart about going with the French agency. It would mean spending more time in glorious Paris while still working in New York, and that was okay with me. A few friends thought I should reconsider, because my new boss had a tainted past in the industry, but that did not bother me. I have never been interested in judging anyone based on their past. We have all sinned and fallen short of the glory of God, including myself.

My job was to lead by example. So I accepted the position.

Not long after I started, my boss came to me with an amazingly beautiful model from Eastern Europe. She had skin like golden butter, but she was looking to leave the agency because she felt she was not getting the right management. My boss was hoping I could convince her to stay.

What a way to start.

But it was also a challenge. I was going to fight to keep this beautiful model with my new agency. She had the look of a model worth millions, and I would need her if I were going to make the agency more successful. The agency represented some of the most beautiful models I had even seen, but no one seemed to understand how to market and place them with the right clients. Girls with star quality were doing basic catalog work with a little editorial thrown in. They were capable of so much more!

My boss and I sat down with this beautiful girl, Greta, and I outlined my vision for her career. She wanted to make money, of course, but she also wanted to do some great editorial work. I was willing to deliver whatever she requested, within reason. I told her that in my judgment, she had a great face for cosmetics and a wonderful body for lingerie, but her hair was not so great for a hair contract. I suggested that we bet on the "trifecta effect" with her and told her that with her help, I could get her three amazing deals within one year: a cosmetics contract, shooting Victoria's Secret and a hair contract.

It was a huge promise, but I had faith that God would help me to deliver.

I was hoping for a year, but Greta agreed to give me a few months to prove what I could do. I accepted; I was willing to gamble that my vision would work within the time frame she had in mind. I knew that if I delivered at least one of the three deals within those first few months, she would give me the leeway to continue for the rest of the year. I saw greatness in her, and I was willing to work three times harder than usual to avoid losing her.

The only one of the three promises that she thought would be impossible to meet was the hair campaign. She had lost all other jobs related to hair, and other agents had told her that she could forget about hair campaigns because her hair was not thick enough. But I hate to hear the word "can't," and I was eager to prove the other agents wrong.

Now I had to find a way to deliver on my promise. I began by researching every advertising agency to see which ones were working on cosmetics projects. Within the first couple of months, as promised, I was negotiating a cosmetics deal for Greta. By the end of the period we had agreed on, she had signed a contract with Max Factor cosmetics and done a shoot for Victoria's Secret.

I had delivered two of the three things I had promised, but I was still not satisfied. I had promised her a hair campaign, and I was determined to deliver. I worked even harder, and by the end of the year we were negotiating a hair contract with a European client for both their print and television campaigns.

After this, Greta trusted me so completely that thoughts of switching agencies never came up again. She started making quite a lot of money and doing some pretty incredible editorial work for some of the top fashion magazines.

God had made sure that my words were honored by delivering all three blessings I had promised. I knew that the peace I had felt when I made those risky pledges had been put in my heart by Him.

Thirteen

BLESSINGS

$\mathcal{O}$ne of my greatest assignments happened during my first few months at the new agency. A lovely young Scandinavian girl, 15 or 16 years of age, became my responsibility. Quiet and shy, with pale, rose-colored skin, jet-black hair, and eyes as innocent as a beautiful young doe, she was the kind of model that needed to be nurtured carefully. I knew that she was special, and I wanted to make sure she was taken good care of—not because she had the potential to become a star but because of her age and being away from her homeland. I had already become a father figure to many of the models I represented, and I treated them all as if they were my own kids, but this was a special one.

I introduced her to one of the industry's top casting directors, who was currently casting a show in Milan for one of the world's leading designers. Immediately, my delicate girl landed an exclusive contract to work for that designer: she would become the face of their campaigns and shows. This was a dream job for any model!

I would have to travel with her to shoots and shows in Europe since she did not have any representation there. All the agencies in Europe wanted her—including the Paris office of my agency—but my boss understood my strategy and the steps I was taking to protect this girl, and he approved what I was doing.

I would sit in my hotel room and schedule her castings, fittings and bookings and make sure she was being safely chauffeured to all her appointments. By now, God's blessings were pouring out everywhere we went. I had full access into the world's leading design houses, sometimes until two or three in the morning. Afterwards, we would head back to our hotel and get a couple of hours of sleep before hitting the streets of Paris again to do shows. On other days, we would go to the studios where she would be photographed for whichever magazine was on the schedule.

If she did not want to do a show, fitting or shoot, I would always make sure that she was excused from the job without the client knowing why. She and I developed an incredible bond; she would confide in me, knowing that I would not disclose anything about her private life to the other agents. During one of the show seasons, we flew her mom and younger brother in from Sweden to witness her walk the runways—something they had never seen her do before. I was excited to see the joy on their faces.

However, I felt in my heart that she was not really enjoying herself or the business. While other models would get excited about shooting *Vogue* or doing a top designer show, she seemed nonchalant about the whole thing. I loved her attitude—she saw what she did as just a job— but in my heart I also hoped that she would at least take some joy in it.

Finally, I could not escape the feeling that something was terribly wrong with her. I could not put a finger on what it was, so I prayed. I prayed that God would bless and protect her on all her travels, castings and bookings and that the time would come when she would open up more about what was troubling her. I felt in my heart she could not have cared less about all that she had achieved—or even about the world of fashion. I sensed she was doing the work because she wanted to please others but was not happy to be in the industry.

Then one day, while working the collections in Paris, I got a call from her while I was in my room. We had gotten back from doing a fitting and were resting for a while, as we were both exhausted from the constant late nights. I was just settling in after making calls to double-check her schedule for the next day of shows when I got a call from her asking if she could come to my room.

"Of course," I said.

When I opened the door, she was standing in the hallway crying. There was blood all over her arms from deliberate slashes that seemed to have been made by razor blades.

I knew immediately what had happened. She was emotionally distraught, so I brought her into the room and cleaned the blood from her arms, making sure that the cuts were not dangerous. After that, I calmly sat her down, and I listened. No conversation before or since has ever hurt my heart as much.

This lovely girl explained that she did not feel beautiful. She was not happy. I was shocked and surprised. My heart was grieving for her. She was a broken child. She was going through something so terrible that she had mutilated her own body! She needed help.

Rediscovering a Child

Everything needed to stop. The fittings, the shoots, all of it. That was clear.

She was crying and pouring her heart out. All I could do was listen, and I prayed in my heart that God would give me the wisdom to say what He wanted me to say and the courage to help her. My first step was obvious: I cancelled the rest of her bookings and told her that it was time for her to go home and be with her family.

She told me she did not want to quit the business, but I knew that it was time for her to go and be with the people who loved her because of her inner beauty, not her outer beauty. We agreed that she would only come to New York for a few direct bookings or whatever work remained on her contract, but that she would be based at home in Sweden. I also found her a psychotherapist and went with her to her first meeting for support.

In the end, she stayed in Sweden. She needed to be with her family and not in this industry. She needed to remain a child and grow up like any normal teenager would, without the pressure of being perfect. All the money in the world was not worth the alternative.

It was clear that the Lord had a strong reason to have me kicked out of the other agency in order to be in a position to help someone else. I had been in a similar situation with mutilation before with my Somali model, and He knew that I was capable of understanding what this young girl was going through. I was able to listen, understand and remind her that she was a gift from God, created in His own image and likeness, no matter what others in fashion thought she should look like.

I was thankful to God that she was able to get out of the business, go back to school and start her life over—to be a child. Some of the agents could not understand why I'd had her quit the business when she could still be making money, but it was the right thing to do. She was more important as a person than as a model.

My Hippie Beauty

And then, a wonderful surprise happened. One day, a beautiful, blonde former Gucci model walked into the agency. She wasn't sure whom she should be meeting, so we all met with her. She had taken about a year off from the industry and gone back home to Canada but had decided to come back. Someone had suggested that she go to an agency on Broadway in SoHo, but she could not find the paper with the address. Making the situation more interesting, next door to our agency was a top agency that was challenging all the major players in the industry by managing only a select few models—including the lady I had gotten into *Vogue Italia* at my old agency before my former boss had ended my contract.

Fortunately, she had chosen to walk into our building!

We were excited. She was a gift brought directly to us. She and I liked each other immediately, and as I had with so many other models, I set my mind to taking care of her. I wanted to get her back into the kind of elite work she had done before walking away from the industry. In talking with her, I found out that one of the reasons she had left the business was due to fluctuations in her weight; her former agency had put tremendous pressure on her to lose weight and stay slim.

I had seen what the pressure to be perfect had done to other models, and I vowed that I would not let it get to her. Because she was not rail-thin, as so many models are, it was obvious that the best way to market her was to go to clients such as *Sports Illustrated* and Victoria's Secret, who liked their models to be beautiful but also to have curves.

The other challenge with this model was that she had a "hippie" mentality. That meant that she would sometimes disappear for weeks or even months when the mood took her. I'm sure some of her past agents found this unbearable, because you never knew if she was in town for a booking. Strangely enough, she and I had a deep understanding of one another. I have always loved working with girls with independent spirits—you never knew what they were going to do next or where they would go—and it was the same with her. I knew how grueling fashion work would be, and I wanted my models to enjoy themselves and not take the industry so seriously that they ended up losing themselves in it.

I set out to get her the clients I had in mind. It was not hard; she immediately booked shoots with both *Sports Illustrated* and Victoria's Secret.

Later, she revealed to me that the agency she was supposed to have met with on the day she walked into our office was actually the agency next door! But by then, she was happy working with us and loved our relationship. It's amazing how God works, making sure to send people into our lives that help us shine. Someone else's loss had become our gain.

A different situation occurred during the same time when we were sent a beautiful model from an agency in London. She was reminiscent of a young Sophia Loren: born in Mexico, with dark hair and blue eyes. She was not tall by model standards, barely 5' 8", but she had stunning, exotic features. Our president was not too keen on representing her because of her height, but another agent—a woman named Carolina—demanded that she and I be allowed to represent her, and he relented.

I was grateful that Carolina was so forceful, because right after we signed the Mexican model, she signed an exclusive contract to be the face of Yves Saint Laurent. Things were starting to happen—and happen fast.

Creative Risk Takers

God had placed me with some great young agents who made my job even more exciting. They knew their duties and were willing to work hard to make sure the agency succeeded. It was a time of great creativity, including working with a great young agency president who was willing to give us freedom to take risks. This made going to work a joy.

Our team was young, and they took joy in their work. We held meetings with clients as a team. Each person knew his or her strengths and weaknesses, and we balanced each other. This led us to another big, exclusive deal. We had moved our offices to 14th Street and Fifth Avenue, to a large, loft-like studio with a deck at the back where the models and agents would have coffee or smoke cigarettes. Because of the amount of stress involved in the business, nicotine and caffeine is part of the industry.

Into this new office came a Danish model that had been with the agency that had been next door to us. With her long, lean legs and megawatt personality, she was an incredible charmer. I guess she felt she needed to be with a smaller agency, even though by now we were doing as much great work as some of the bigger agencies that had been around for a long time. We had girls with exclusive contracts and great editorial work in *Vogue*, *Harper's Bazaar* and all the other major magazines. We had surpassed my former agency in every way, with bigger star models and larger contracts.

Within six months, the Danish model was doing the Gucci show in Milan and then signing an exclusive contract to be their model. Every model dreams of having an exclusive contract that brings financial security, keeps them in the spotlight and lets them work with the top photographers and magazines. In several years with her old agency, she had not made it to the next level, but our agency was able to figure out how to position her and what clients to position her with.

It was incredibly gratifying to see her success. She went on to star in feature films and is now a top young film director.

How to Dress to Make $10,000 a Day

Image is important for anyone wanting to succeed in fashion. It is the staple of the industry.

A great model has to do more than look great on camera or the catwalk; she (or he) must be able to inspire the client, whether that is a designer, editor, photographer or agent. A model that can do so quickly rises to the top of the industry. Such models become super-models. They become rock stars.

Few models have the drive or tenacity to go that far. Instead, they settle for what they are content with. Supermodels like Naomi, Linda, Christy, Kate, Heidi, and Gisele (notice that you know them all by their first names) have one thing in common over all the others: they command attention. If you're in a room full of people and any one of these women walks in, you will stop what you're doing and notice them. It doesn't matter if they are wearing jeans and flip-flops. They have an air about them that is unmatched. Their smiles, walk, speech and everything else about them set them apart from everyone else. They can set a room on fire.

But while image is important in fashion, with God the heart is more important. If your heart is right with Him, you will always want to look good not only outside but inside. You will be an ambassador of His and want to be your best. To those models that would listen, I have always given a piece of good advice: dress like you are worth $10,000 a day and you will earn that much. Dress like you're not and you will settle for less.

You don't have to spend a lot of money to look great. Buy simple, classic pieces at designer sample sales, mix them with an expensive pair of shoes and a great bag or belt (buying these is an investment in your business), and voila! That can make a huge difference in how people perceive you in any industry—which in the end can make you look like you're worth more than you are..

Case in point: we were representing a 5'10" exotic beauty that went on to marry a famous action film star. She was a wonderful girl—well educated, smart and lovely—and she had the potential to become a star but was very reserved in her manner. She had been raised as a Catholic schoolgirl type, well bred and mannerly. She was a perfect example of someone who had not appeared in *Vogue* but who had the potential to be a *Vogue* model (years later she would end up in the pages of both *Vogue* & *W*).

I explained to her that the way that she dressed could influence how other people—including stylists, photographers and designers— saw her. Being smart, she understood immediately, and she upgraded her attitude and style. Practically overnight, her earnings went from a few thousand dollars a day to between $10,000 and 15,000 per day for catalog shoots. It was incredible. She had not changed as a model, but she had taken control of how others perceived her. Because of this, she went from making $200,000 a year to more than $1,000,000 per year.

Sadly, we've also had models with the same physical beauty that refused to invest in themselves and "dress the part." Inevitably, they ended up making much less money and enjoying fewer opportunities. Refusing to dress the part and act the part can cost us in life. In fashion, you are who others believe you to be.

The Red-Eyed Monster

While blessings flowed our way daily, one of the curses I dealt with regularly was envy between models. I was working with a beautiful mixed-race model from the Caribbean. She consistently made several hundred thousand dollars a year just working in Miami; she had a niche market, and she was doing well in it.

But my lovely beauty from the islands had all the symptoms of what in Jamaica is known as "red eye." In this context, "red eye" wasn't a virus. It refers to someone who is envious of what someone else has. Americans call it the "green-eyed monster," but in either culture, the term describes someone who is envious of others, greedy, lustful and has eyes like the devil.

When my island model started working in New York, she saw another model of mixed heritage with hair totally different from hers. This French model's hair was longer and with large ringlets while the model from the island had shorter hair. Both models were doing well in their own right—until the day the island girl showed up at the agency with hair extensions similar to the French model's. We were appalled; we all loved the island girl's hair because it was unique and exciting. It made her stand out from the many other models that had long ringlets.

"You've got red eyes," I told her.

She stood there, not sure what to say but knowing full well what I meant. She had been doing well with her own special style but was abandoning that style in order to emulate someone else.

What I said was not nice. Since I was representing the Lord in words and in deeds, I was always careful to be gentle, kind and loving. But I was shocked at what she had done with her hair, and I needed to shock her into realizing what she had done.

She changed her hair back to the beautiful locks she had before. Later, I asked God for forgiveness.

At the other extreme of the hair spectrum was Margreet. She was a sweet, unassuming Swedish blonde who had been working as a commercial model, doing mostly catalog work. She was no longer one of the younger models that agents scampered around trying to represent, redevelop or market to the top clients. She was in her mid- or late twenties and considered "too old" for the superstar clients. "Sweet Margreet" had missed the boat for *Vogue* and was relegated to "B" and "C" clients.

However, Sweet Margreet wanted to give *Vogue* one more shot. Now that she was a hen, she was going to claw her way out of the young chicken coop, out from under all the underage models with their fresh-as-a-daisy cheeks and try to snag a high-level campaign. I loved her spirit and drive, so I decided to help her.

Unlike my island model with her hair disaster, Margreet turned her hair into an asset. She had it lightened and chopped with bangs, giving her an edgy feel that was amazing. She looked stunning. The quiet, sweet old Margreet, who had thought her days of *Vogue* were over, became one of the most sought-after models in the agency—a modern, sexy model amongst a group of skinny young chickens.

I went into overdrive promoting and booking her. I took some Polaroids and, with a note attached, sent them over to the studio of one of *Vogue's* top photographers. The call came within hours: they wanted to see her immediately. She was booked to appear in the campaign for Versace's younger Versus line! The "too old" model had her day and showed the young chickens what being a model was about. She proved to many agents that she could be just as beautiful, edgy and interesting as any young model on the market.

Dear Lord, we've all had "red eyes" at some point in our lives. Help me to keep from accusing anyone else of jealously or envy until I have left those qualities behind myself.

Fourteen

The Beginning of the End

September 11, 2001 began like any other day. I was getting ready to go to work—not a difficult thing for me, as I lived only a few blocks from the agency.

I was having a cup of tea and watching Katie Couric of NBC interviewing Harry Belafonte about the AIDS problem in Africa when the news broke about the first plane flying into the World Trade Center. My first reaction was the same as everyone else's: shock and horror! I prayed that everyone would be okay.

They weren't. The live news broadcast showed the next plane slamming into the second tower, and I knew that my adopted country was under attack. I started praying, not only for the people on the plane but also for their families, our nation and its leaders. I walked to the agency to make sure everyone there was okay. Along the way, I saw the faces of neighbors and strangers; they were in total shock, crying and hugging each other, and trying to comfort those who could not cope with what had just happened.

I've always been calm in extreme situations, but this was the most difficult situation I've ever encountered. At the agency, I received a phone call from a French reporter asking me to give my response to what was happening. I had no idea what to say; I didn't know any more than anyone else. By this time, there had been an attack on the Pentagon, along with the plane that went down in a field in Pennsylvania.

At this time, I had not thought much about my friend and former roommate, Michael Richards. We had last seen each other about two months earlier. My friend Chelsea, who worked with me when I had my own agency, had introduced me to Michael years earlier at a barbecue on the roof of his apartment building, and we immediately became friends.

An artist, Michael was used to having roommates share his duplex loft (formerly a monastery) on 15th Street, so I was excited when Chelsea told me that his former roommate had moved out and that he would be looking for another one. I was living on Montague Street off the promenade in Brooklyn Heights, but I wanted to live closer to my work. To be able to move back into the city would be a great blessing.

So I rented the second bedroom in Michael's apartment, which meant less time on the subway and more time walking the streets of New York. Perhaps I would spot another beautiful future model!

Well, Michael's name was still on the lease, and at dinner he and I had discussed becoming roommates again. I had received an email from him just a few weeks back to say hello and update me on his work. He was a great friend and such a dedicated artist that he would stay up late working on projects for shows in the city and around the world. I even introduced him to one of my former models, and they hit it off. They even became engaged.

Then, suddenly, things went sour. The bride called off the wedding. Michael was shattered. My fun-loving friend became sad and depressed. To compound matters, his mother was diagnosed with terminal cancer. During her illness, he moved into his parents' home in Queens so that he would be able to take her to her doctor and still commute to the city to work on his art. About a year later, his mom died.

Now, on September 11, no one had heard from Michael.

The first sign that something was very wrong came when I received an email from a girl that knew us both asking if I had heard from Michael. I hadn't. I called his cell phone and got his voicemail. I left a message but received no response. I kept calling all day, but every time, it went straight to voice mail. Now I was becoming frightened.

Then I remembered that he had been working on a project for the City of New York.

A couple of years earlier, his career had taken off, with showings around the country and in Europe. Then the city had commissioned some New York artists to work on some projects and had let them use studio space in the Twin Towers. Michael had a fascination with airplanes and was commissioned to create sculptures dedicated to the Tuskegee Airmen, a group of black pilots who fought in World War II.

It was possible that he could have been working in the Towers, I thought.

I started contacting all his other friends and checking around. His ex-fiancé and I went on a campaign, putting up posters around the city asking, "Have you seen Michael Richards?" But we were beginning to realize the horrible truth. Then, the inevitable happened: we had been putting flyers up on Fifth Avenue around Eighth and Ninth—on the fence of a beautiful chapel—when a lady came after us asking if we knew Michael.

"Of course," I said, hoping for some good news but also not sure what to expect. She went on to say that she was his half-sister, had given birth to a baby a few months earlier, and that her husband (who worked in the World Trade Center) was also missing.

My heart went out to her. I had not known that Michael had any siblings, but his ex-fiancé confirmed that it was true. Michael's so-called sister said that she had constantly been checking with an information center not far away to see if there had been any word from hospitals or morgues about the identities of bodies recovered from the wreckage of the towers. I was happy to get any help or information, and she agreed to take us to the place where we could check to see if there was any information on my friend.

Deception and Tragedy

The information center had no word on him, so I decided to head home and figure out my next move the following day. However,

Michael's sister told me that she was stuck in the city because there were no vehicles going into or coming out of the New Jersey tunnels. I immediately offered her my apartment for the night, saying something like, "A sister of Michael's is family of mine."

She thanked me, gave God glory, and came back to my apartment with me. When we arrived, I called Michael's father in the Caribbean to let him know that I had his son's half-sister on the line. I immediately passed the phone to her without waiting to hear what he had to say. I figured this was a difficult time for them both since it was now Thursday and there was still no word from Michael; I didn't want to eavesdrop on their conversation.

I had another friend staying in the apartment's back room, so I decided to give his sister my bedroom while I slept on the sofa. In the morning, I had a strange feeling that someone was standing over me. I opened my eyes, and there was Michael's sister, standing over me and looking quite strange. I was quite taken aback so I said something like, "Did you sleep well?"

She answered, "I was hoping to wake you up," which did not make sense. She then told me that she was going to meet with a museum curator friend of Michael's to see if she had any information. Something did not seem right, but since she knew so much about Michael, I ignored the feeling. Once again, I would regret not listening to God's still, small voice.

She and the museum curator had agreed to meet at the Episcopal Church on Seventh Avenue and 13th Street, as she said that she wanted to go and pray. But once inside they sat about seven pews ahead of me. This was becoming stranger and stranger.

That was when I started feeling uncomfortable in my stomach. To compound everything, it started raining so I excused myself and told them that I had to go home. By the time I got to my place a few blocks away, I was sick to my stomach. The stress of trying to find Michael and not knowing if he was alive, having two guests staying in my apartment, and hearing all the news about the thousands possibly dead or injured had finally taken a toll on my body.

I decided to stay home and get some sleep.

I woke up on Saturday morning early with the certainty that Michael was dead. I decided that I would call his sister to see how she was doing, but the two telephone numbers she had given me were disconnected. Instantly, I felt that sense that something was not right. I knew I would never see her again. Most importantly, I figured that she was not who she had claimed to be.

That evening, Michael's dad arrived from the Caribbean, and we agreed to meet the next day because he had to go down and do DNA testing. There were many bodies found badly damaged, and the authorities were hoping that DNA from family members might help them identify the dead.

After Mr. Richards got his swab test, he asked, "Who was that lady you put on the phone Thursday night?"

I replied, "Michael's half-sister."

He looked at me calmly and said, "His half-sister is in Canada."

Yikes!

Mr. Richards explained to me that he had no idea who that woman had been. She most definitely had not been Michael's half-sister. It did not take me long to figure out who she was.

A few days later, the police called my apartment looking to speak to me. Apparently, the woman pretending to be Michael's half-sister had been arrested in Queens. In her possession were two of my credit cards and details about my finances. She was a scam artist and an identity thief!

I filed a report about all that happened and then contacted the credit card company. They gave me a detailed description of all the charges she had put on my account, including a shopping spree and a trip to the manicurist with the "museum curator." But the saddest part was that the cop told me that there had been many scams targeting people like myself who had lost someone in the tragedy.

The charges to my credit accounts totaled about $1,600, but that paled next to the fact that DNA testing had identified

Michael's body. Losing money was not important; losing a friend was a tragedy. I would have paid any amount of money to get him back.

Michael Richards was buried with a closed casket.

The Monster

After the attacks on our country and my friend's death, life took a different path for me. I no longer had the desire for more *Vogue*, Gucci or Versace. I sought the Lord more than ever and kept looking to Him to guide me.

I was still going to work hard to give my models and the agency what I was being paid to do, but I would no longer tolerate petty, silly, greedy, selfish tantrums from models or clients. I would ignore them or walk away and accept the impact on my career.

With the tremendous success of the agency, many doors were opening. Many different kinds of models were seeking us out and asking us to represent them, including one hot new model that was becoming famous for appearing in *Sports Illustrated* and Victoria's Secret. Apparently, this model had been represented by the agency a few years earlier and made only about $1,500 per day. She was let go but went on to be represented by another agency that took the time to nurture her and deliver her dreams by getting her both the swimsuit and lingerie campaigns. Despite her success at that other agency, she felt she was not being managed properly by them, and she had asked someone to contact me and set up a meeting. She thought that I could help take her to another level. She was willing to switch back to our agency if I would represent her.

I do not like to take models from other agencies deliberately. I had done it before, and each time I felt God's rebuke in my heart. This time was no different. But after a few calls from her, we met. I explained to her that it would be best if she sat down with her current agency (which turned out to be my old "spiders and snakes" agency) and talk to them about her problems and questions before making a decision. I told her that if she felt that things had not changed after about three months, she should come back and see me.

About two months later she called me for another meeting. She told me that she was ready to switch because she had not been booked with her two major clients—*Sports Illustrated* and Victoria's Secret—in a long time and had feared that she might be on the verge of losing them. At this point, I felt that it was reasonable to take her on.

I became her agent and decided to do the best I could to restore her image and retain her key clients. Within eleven months she was making $15,000 to $30,000 per day and had won back her two main clients. She was ecstatic and told me so. Then the bomb dropped!

She would be employing a publicist to help build up her image. That wasn't a bother to me, even though I thought it was a bit odd since she was already getting lots of free press from promoting the *Sports Illustrated* annual Swimsuit Issue. But it was not my money; if she chose to spend it on publicity that was her business. Then, one day, she decided that we all needed to meet her publicist to discuss strategies on how to increase her visibility. I thought *Isn't that supposed to be the publicist's job?*

The president and I sat in the meeting with the model and her publicist and listened to what they had to say. Then, with a straight face, the publicist said the following: our girl was becoming more famous and more loved than the world's biggest supermodel, Naomi Campbell!

I thought it was a joke. She could not be serious. This model was bigger than the most in-demand face in the fashion world?

I stifled my laughter, but in my shock I said something like, "Are you serious? Surely, you're joking."

This did not go over well. The agency president sat there a little bewildered, but he kept calm. The publicist went on and on. The entire time, my star model sat there, believing the baloney that her publicist was dishing out. I thought, *These two cannot possibly believe what they are saying.* Someone needed to give them a reality check.

But they were serious. With difficulty, I kept my composure, listened and then wished them God's blessings.

Pride always goeth before a fall. This woman was not satisfied with her success; she wanted more and she wanted it now! After they left, the agency president and I had a good laugh about what we had heard.

Then the drama began. She was booked to appear in a famous singer's music video and had agreed to do it for $30,000. However, the night before the shoot we received a phone call from the producer of the video. Our model's publicist had called them with some demands, including giving our model her own trailer along with special food, water, service and more. Not surprisingly, the producer was furious.

Then at around one in the morning, another call came in. It was the publicist stating that she wanted the model's call time changed from 9:00am to 3:00pm. Who phones in the middle of the night to make these kinds of demands?

Their egos were out of control, and God was warning me in a loud voice about what was to come. Fortunately, I had learned to listen. After the video, I found out that our model had started shopping for another agency. I was with a former co-worker, walking in the West Village, when we saw another agent we knew from London. This agent told me that our young would-be Naomi Campbell and her pet publicist had come to meet with his agency—along with one of my former bosses—to discuss signing with them. According to our friend, both the model and my ex-boss outlined what the model had achieved (due, of course, to all the work that we had done for her) and said that they felt she could do even more.

The agency's response: "What more could we do than your current agency has already done?" They declined to represent her. It's always best when an unhappy model leaves an agency. I prefer to work with people who are happy with the work we're doing for them than to have disgruntled, miserable people sitting around complaining and poisoning things for everyone.

Our president thought we should fight to keep her—or at least confront her. In general, it is best to let people know that you're onto their games. I left her a few messages, but she did not respond. The president made plans to confront her at one of the bookings that we had gotten for her.

I didn't think this was a good idea. It was, after all, someone's place of work. Finally, she agreed to come in and meet with us—individually, rather than together as a team. Divide and conquer. She spoke first with the president and thanked him for the great job he had done for her, when in fact everyone knew that he had not done any of the work that had made her successful.

Then it was my turn. She sat down wearing large dark shades. Quite a fashion statement, but more important, she did not want me to see into her eyes. Supermodel legs crossed, she kept the big dark shades on. Next, her head started bopping from side to side.

Good grief, call an exorcist, I thought.

If I could have seen her eyes—I was convinced they would have been fire engine red. I had no idea if she was tormented, demented or just being dramatic. Of course, she wasn't the devil or a demon. She was just possessed...by something.

There was no priest around to throw holy water on her in case her head started spinning, her eyes started bulging, or she started speaking in another tongue. So I decided to pray. What else could I do?

While her head kept bopping from side to side, she said, "I came to this agency because of you, and I'm leaving because of you."

God bless you, I thought. *You're leaving. Praise the Lord!*

She would be leaving with lots of money in her pockets. I was happy to see her go somewhere else and try to dethrone Naomi. In my opinion, she could never go toe-to-toe with Naomi, but I would let her find that out for herself. There was nothing more for me to say.

I stood up, extended my hand to her, and like a gentleman, sincerely thanked her for coming to the agency and giving us all the opportunity to work with her. The Lord giveth and the Lord taketh away, and bless Him for taking her away!

At that moment, she started shaking. I realized that she was shocked at my reaction. I was not going to beg her to stay!

I was looking at a monster I had helped to create, and I did not like what I was seeing. The industry that I loved had become a madness of overpaid, self-indulgent people who were not thankful for their blessings. We weren't saving lives nor were we a medical team helping others. She was just a highly paid clothes hanger, and I had been her pimp of an agent.

It amazes me how quickly a person can change from not having much to having a lot—and how this can change their attitude toward others. To me, it's wise not to look too hard at old boxes of shoes, as you may see a pair that you once liked and will end up keeping in your closet, even though you know in your heart that you won't ever wear them again.

Michael's death had infused me with a harsh sense of reality, and I was relieved and elated to let go of this "old shoe." I'm not sure what her eyes were doing behind the dark shades, but I'm glad I could not see them. I can't remember saying anything else to her. I smiled politely then walked back to my desk, leaving her sitting in the office, stunned. It is always wise not to say too much. Keep it simple and walk away without looking back.

No amount of money was worth the drama that would have afflicted the agency if she had stayed with us. The commissions were not worth the headache. We would have become slaves to her every whim. As you can guess, she ended up at another agency with the promise that she would become bigger than Naomi. It didn't happen.

She was left with a group of agents who did not believe in her or her publicist's hype. From the $15,000 to $30,000 per day she had been making with us, she dropped to a mere $5,000 to $7,500. That was proof to me that it is important to be thankful and realistic about your life—to know the difference between hype and blessings from God. Ego and pride are the two ugliest accessories any model can ever wear.

Falling Down

During this time, God had been preparing another model with a more thankful, humble attitude.

One of our agents had gone scouting in London and found a beautiful model that he thought I would love to work with. He was right. The moment he showed me her Polaroid sheet, I knew I needed to have her in the city immediately.

There was something magical yet simple about this woman with her nonchalant attitude that won us over. It was agreed that we would represent her. It was refreshing to work with someone who made no demands but instead trusted that we would work hard on her behalf. Once in New York, she gained the attention of the top photographers, editors and designers and ended up doing a shoot for *Vogue*. Then she was booked to do the Gucci show in Milan.

The night of the show in Milan, I decided that I did not want to deal with the crowds of people fighting to get in. As in New York or Paris, I was never enamored about seeing the shows, even though I think French and Italian productions tend to be more creative and fun to watch than American shows. I thought it would be best to stay in my Milan hotel room and catch up with my model in the morning over coffee. Perhaps we would just talk on the phone before we headed to Paris.

At about six in the morning, I was awakened by a phone call from the casting director of the Gucci show. I was excited to hear how my model had done the previous night, and when he said, "Your girl was a big hit at the show last night..." I was thrilled! But then I heard the rest of his words and I was tempted to bury my head beneath the sheets.

"She was a hit all right, but in the wrong way!"

What? The casting director went on to tell me that my model had taken several falls on the catwalk, including one where she nearly fell onto the editor-in-chief of *Vogue* and another top editor!

This was horrifying. No way was this happening.

To stumble once down a catwalk is bad, but to keep falling down is startling and humiliating. Something like that could end a career before it even got started. To nearly fall on the two biggest people at *Vogue* was even worse.

I was mortified, but it got worse. He continued, "The editor has someone for her to meet in Paris to help her learn how to walk!"

It turned out that my sneaker-wearing model did not know how to walk in high heels! She had fallen on her face on the biggest stage in the fashion industry.

Suddenly, I started laughing. It was too funny! The casting director laughed a bit, too, and then calmly told me to have my model call the editor at his hotel in Paris.

At least they will always remember her, I told myself.

I tried to go back to sleep after hanging up the phone, but I ended up getting up and wondered how she was doing. I decided to wait until a more respectful hour to call her and discuss what happened.

Well, that young model gave me a great lesson in bravery. As we spoke that morning, she explained that all the models had practiced the choreographed walk—but with braces on with their heels, since they would be walking on a fur-lined stage. She had explained to the producers before the start of the show that she still needed the braces but was told that it would not be possible. So she tried her best to walk in the heels on furs and BAM! Tumbled and stumbled.

She had a great attitude about her fall. She was calm and cool about it, and she even went on to say, "Hey, at least they'll remember me!" I loved the fact that she was so confident and had the right attitude, laughing at herself.

Her fall made news all around the world, and she became known as "the model who kept falling at Gucci," but she didn't let that stop her. Today, she is still a successful model and has added "TV host and comedienne" to her resume. She was one of the good things about a business that by that time had begun to exhaust me.

Dear Lord, thank you for giving me the wisdom and strength to walk away from things—to see the long term and not just the short. I overlooked your signs in the past, but no more. In saying goodbye to my head-shaking model, I finally submitted completely to your will. Amen.

Fifteen

THE FINAL NAIL

The final nail in the coffin that led me to leave the fashion industry came in the form of two fluffy white haired dogs, a stocky older man claiming to be a personal manager, and his Eastern Bloc model, who had long legs, pale skin, black hair, piercing blue eyes covered with sunglasses, and an all-black outfit.

The dogs scampered into the agency, sniffing around for a place to relieve themselves. They were followed by the model, who looked every bit the part. She carried herself as though she lived on Park Avenue or in Trocadero in Paris. Her manager tried not to let anyone know that he was also her husband. It was one of the strangest pairings I had ever seen in the business. But it was not that unusual. I had seen the combination before: beautiful young woman with an older "Svengali" type acting as her manager, mentor, keeper…and oftentimes, lover.

My boss had convinced this odd couple that we could do great things representing them in New York, and he was right. The model was beautiful—absolutely stunning. She also knew how to make an entrance even with her props—dogs and husband—in tow. She had been successful as a model in Europe and had weighed her options before her husband made the decision to have us represent her.

The decision paid off. Within six weeks she had earned more than $187,000 for about twelve days of work. It was a good start for a model working in a totally new market, but it wasn't unprecedented.

Unfortunately, Svengali didn't see it that way. Immediately, the demands began.

First came the demand for a chauffeur-driven car to take her on all her appointments. That was not overly unusual for a model of her stature. But then she started sending back the drivers because of silly things, especially if the car windows were not tinted. After that, her dogs became a nuisance, as they were always looking for a place to relieve themselves when they were in our offices.

In less than six months, this beautiful woman had become the biggest monster in the agency's history. Not even the head-bopping supermodel who had left us was as rude and disrespectful. Her disregard for the agents and assistants reached a point where I knew we had to let her go, even though she was becoming a huge money earner for us. We had learned our lesson and would not allow another diva in the making to ruin our agency. We were over the dogs peeing in corners, the rotund husband making demands, and her arrogant, selfish behavior.

When she made the mistake of claiming that a client should pay for a mistake she had made, that was the excuse we needed. She was booked on a shoot on one of the British Virgin Islands for one of the biggest department stores in the world, making $12,000 per day for four days. I told her that she needed to get a visa; since she was from Eastern Europe, she would definitely need one to enter the country. She told me that she already had a work visa for the UK; I informed her that she would need a different one, since her visa only covered the United Kingdom, not its territories.

In her arrogance, she was certain that she was correct. On the day she was to travel from New York, the airline representative at JFK airport told her that they could not allow her on the flight because she did not have the proper visa. She was angry, blaming everyone at the agency and refusing to accept responsibility for her mistake. In the end, we were able to get her a visa that day so that she could travel out the next morning, but she demanded that the client pay her for the two days of missed work.

That was the end. We knew this relationship was not going to work. We terminated her contract. Her husband started shopping her around town, and in the end she ended up at my old agency working for my former boss after he gave her manager/husband more than $50,000 as an advance on future work. My former boss heard about all the money I had made for this model and figured the advance was a good investment. Surely, she would earn far more!

He was wrong.

She, her husband and the two dogs fled to Paris with the cash my former boss gave them and disappeared, never to return. To this day, I don't think they ever returned a cent, but good riddance.

Closing the Door

My thoughts of walking away from the fashion business had been brewing for a while. For years, I'd kept working because I was being paid very well for doing something that I found quite easy. But I wasn't a brain surgeon. I wasn't saving lives. I hoped that I had made a positive impact on the models, clients and fellow co-workers I worked with throughout the years; that was all I could hope for.

I was called a booker or agent, but, in reality, I was a hustler. I was paid handsomely to make the models and my bosses lots of money. Well, money doesn't always bring joy, peace or contentment. It can buy some cool designer pieces but not inner peace. There's a peace that comes from above, and it had been tugging at my heart, telling me to "let go and walk away." For the past few years I had been holding on, but deep down in my heart I knew that if I did not leave, I would be pushed out again.

Then God gave me a push.

On a cold, brisk winter evening in early February 2003, my boss called a staff meeting to discuss the progress of the agency. This was quite normal for him, since he was never able to make it to the agency in the mornings due to his late-night social activities. But this meeting was different from the others. He was like a squirrel scampering up and down a catwalk. He was on a tirade, and the majority of it appeared to be directed at me.

For the past year I had kept a promise: I would complete my contract and not switch to another agency. One morning months earlier, my boss had called me at home to inform me that he was about to fire the agency president, who was also a fellow agent. Even though I did not have the formal title, I was the agency vice president, and my boss wanted my assurance that I would not leave the agency after the president's departure. I gave him my promise that I would see out the remainder of my contract.

At that point, however, I knew that I did not want to work as an agent anymore. Deep in my heart, I was already making plans to leave the business for good at the end of my contract. I was tired of the same routine, discovering new talent and chasing after *Vogue*. I was bored, and I knew it was time to follow the clouds that I felt were drifting away from me.

I also knew that I was bringing quite a lot of money into the agency and that if my contract was renewed, my salary would probably approach that of the president. So I was happy to also keep my options open, just in case.

Not knowing any of this, my boss did what he thought was best for his agency. When I arrived at the agency that morning, after being informed that the president was being fired, I found that all the locks on the door had been changed. *That was quick*, I thought. I guess they had done it in the middle of the night.

The office manager was at the door to meet me. With her glasses perched on her nose like a Catholic schoolteacher, she told me that my fellow agent (and president of the agency) had already been called and told not to return to the office. Now I understood. Without the president's big salary, I had nothing to negotiate with, or against, in case I decided to stay for an extra year. It was very shrewd of my boss, and it was a clear sign that there was no need for me to hang around any longer.

Divorce

However, until my contract ran out, I would remain focused on the models. Many had left the agency to go to the new agency formed by our ex-president. Some of my fellow agents followed him to his new agency, taking even more high-profile models with them. My boss retaliated with a slew of lawsuits. Then the ex-president asked me to join him at his newly formed agency, but I declined. I knew I was over the business. Also, I still had time remaining on my contract and was going to honor it.

What I really wanted was a divorce. My marriage to fashion was over. I felt sad for both my boss and the ex-president because we had started to build an incredible agency, but ego and ugly negotiation tactics had cost us some truly talented young agents and models. But even if I had wanted to, I could not walk away and leave my boss lying flat on his face. I would continue working to help rebuild the agency's image and make sure the models knew that they were in a safe environment, until my contract was up.

Then, three or four months after the president had been locked out of the agency, I was asked to lunch with my boss and the comptroller of the company. *Lord, not another restaurant firing*, I thought. But as soon as the thought came, it went. It wasn't the last day of my contract, so something else was up. I felt a wonderful sense of peace because I knew I had worked harder than ever, with fewer hands on deck, to keep the agency financially strong. I knew God's favor was on my life and work, and it showed with the bookings and money coming in.

On the way to the restaurant, my boss and the comptroller told me they wanted me to meet someone who would be coming on board to help with bookings. "Is he the new president?" I asked.

They both said nothing. So, I asked again.

My boss started to give me a spiel: he was young, energetic and would be a great addition. Still, he did not answer my question, so I said, "If he's the president, that's cool. Just let me know!" There was no need to avoid answering the question; it was going to come out anyway. I wanted to know who it was, but they wouldn't say.

At the restaurant, a lanky young man who was trying to look fashionable—maybe someone who had once wanted to be a model but never quite made it—shook my hand and said something about it being a "pleasure to meet me." He had heard about my reputation in the industry and was looking forward to working with me.

Sure. Whatever. *Let's eat!* I thought.

I replied, "It's a pleasure meeting you, too!"

He seemed like a nice young man, but I had been around the block a few times and had never heard his name mentioned by anyone in the industry. However, since I did not know many agents other than the ones I had worked with and a few famous ones, I figured that he had to have been around for at least a few years to be given such a position.

But it was not my company, and I had only another six months left on my contract, so I was not going to be bothered.

We had a nice little lunch, but it was disrespectful of my boss to consider someone else as president when I was the vice president. I had not told them that I was planning to leave, so it was a surprise that they would seek out someone else without having the decency to say something to me. I didn't care about a job that I no longer wanted, but I still wanted to be treated with respect.

I reminded myself that there is no such thing as loyalty in the fashion world. Nor, for that matter, is there decency.

I was not angry with the young man; he had nothing to do with what was happening. He had obviously talked a good game, and they bought it. But the poor fellow had no clue what to do when he started work at the agency. He had never worked in a major agency or with any top models before, and he didn't know that the work could be ruthless and demanding. He didn't even know anything about the booking table or how the system worked.

It was quite obvious that he had done none of the things he had claimed to have done or worked at the places where he had claimed to work. You would have thought someone would have checked out his credentials first before hiring him, but that hadn't happened.

So I spent a week educating our new president on how to be an agent and then another week teaching him how to manage an agency. He was lost and scared like a deer in a photographer's spotlights.

By the third week, he was gone. Even the people who had been foolish enough to hire him knew better than to pay him for sitting around.

No More Drama

With my boss's actions leaving a sour taste in my mouth, I wanted out and fast. To keep my mind focused on the models for the remaining time of my contract, I put blinders on, as a jockey would put on his horse to keep him looking ahead, and I kept booking as much business as I could.

Then a sign came from above via the music business: Mary J. Blige's new hit song, "No More Drama"! It became my anthem. Unconsciously, I was starting to sing my swan song. It became a joke in the agency: whenever the song started playing on the radio, I would sing and hum along with it.

I was preparing myself to walk away—toward God—and now I had a daily reminder from Mary to banish drama from my life.

By the fall of that year, when my contract was up, I had not renewed my deal. I had a ten percent ownership in the company that my attorney had negotiated that had not been implemented. By signing a new deal, with part ownership of the company on top of the salary I would be making, I would make a lot more money!

I didn't care. I wanted out.

By Christmas, I was in the beautiful Dominican Republic with two other agents, enjoying a break from the industry. I was on the same island a month earlier, celebrating Thanksgiving with an editor friend, and I had felt in my heart that God was showing me it was time to walk away from being an agent. By Christmas I knew that it was time to go.

I was tired and burnt out. I was bored. There was no challenge anymore. It had become too easy. The calm breeze and turquoise Caribbean waters gave me time to sit and consider my next move. Because I had not renewed my contract, I was technically a "free agent." I could leave at any time. A few months had passed since my contract's expiration, but I had deliberately not raised the issue with my boss. He had not brought it up either, which was cool with me.

As I celebrated the beginning of 2003 on that glorious island, I confided in one of the agents that I planned to leave by June. I wanted to have enough money in my bank account to travel for quite a while without having to look for another job until God directed me to do so. I figured I would go to Brazil or one of the many places I enjoyed and start over, even though I had no clue what I wanted to do.

As the New Year rolled in, I headed back to New York and settled myself back into the agency life. I was not happy to be back; my clouds had moved on, and I was lagging behind, watching them go by while sitting in my pasture of an agency, miserable. But I was going to stick with the plan and stay on until June.

I had felt the same thing before, when I knew the clouds had moved: when I had to close my own agency, when I left Carmen's agency, and when I had been pushed out on my backside at Il Tre Merli. I knew that despite this feeling, I had to continue working hard to make sure that I was being a blessing to the models and not taking my boss's money without doing a great job.

Then, on that fateful day in early February, while I listened to my boss ranting and raving about the company at one of his impromptu meetings, I started to pray. In that moment, I felt in my heart a still, quiet voice saying, "How much longer will you continue to be humiliated by these ungrateful people?"

Wow, that was clear!

At that moment an incredible surge of peace came over me. I had worked hard and stayed faithful—even when they brought that joker of a new president on board and did not give me the ownership share that I was owed.

At that moment, I knew in my heart what God had been trying to show me for the last couple of years. This time I was going to obey Him.

I smiled inside. Mine would not be a June departure, but an immediate one. A few days later, I went in to give my boss my notice of resignation. He wasn't in; he had flown off to Brazil. However, I was not going to wait. I called a meeting with one of the financial backers from our Paris office—and the comptroller. They thought I was going to bring up my ten percent ownership share, and they began our meeting by promising that they would have the paperwork ready for me to sign in a few days.

I thanked them and told them that it was not necessary anymore. I was resigning, effective immediately.

They were shocked. But I was not interested in owning an agency. I was only interested in growing my faith and continuing to trust God in everything. I had given my word that I would not leave until my contract had been up. Now, it was up. When God speaks in our hearts, it is best not to question His plans.

Departure

When it became clear that I was serious, they asked me to stay for three weeks, until the end of February, and not to say anything to the other agents, models or clients until they could find a replacement for me. They did not want to disrupt the booking table by having models defect to other agencies.

I complied. I kept quiet about my plans, telling only my mom and the friend who had been with me in the Dominican Republic. But I felt great. My bags were packed! There would be no looking back!

On the final day of February 2003, I shook the dust off, smiled and scampered down the stairs. There was a patch of cloud to catch up with. God always has a cloud ready to lead us. Mine was waiting!

I could see it in the distance, saying, "Bom dia, Brazil!"

Truly, the Lord was and is still my Agent.

Dear Lord, I've finally run the race you asked me to, and now you are releasing me from my bondage. Please forgive me for the harsh and lavish words I have written about the people I have worked with. I truly love each and every one of them. They are your children, just as I am.

But, I'm getting away!

Very far away!

Please let someone else do the babysitting.

Amen!

Afterword

A NOTE OF GRATITUDE

As an agent, you see thousands of models. I'm sure I don't remember them all, even some I've represented myself. However, I still receive emails and letters from many of the models I have represented over the years. Most often, they thank me for taking care of them or encouraging them during times of trial and doubt. Some of these models I may have only seen or represented for a short period of time, since models and agents alike tend to switch agencies constantly. There is often no time to form close relationships with all of them.

However, with each model I was blessed to represent, I'm thankful to God for that opportunity. My heart didn't care if the model was a Christian, Muslim, Jew, black, white, Indian, or anything else. I loved managing models who did not look like the people other agents were representing. I did not want to follow the crowd, and I was blessed to have the gift of vision, enabling me to choose models that others had overlooked and create something beautiful with the ones I represented.

To all my former bosses, thank you! Thank you for being the tools and vessels God used to open so many doors for me: for granting me the opportunity to open your hearts, agencies and your wallets, for paying me well, for letting me do what I loved. You fed not only me through all the lessons I learned, but many others as well.

Each day as I stepped out the door of my apartment to go to work, I became a different person, navigating in my mind how I would make my models successful. My mind would race over what needed to be done, who needed to be called, who needed more attention, who needed an extra push and who needed someone to listen to the things they cared about. During those years, I had to let go of any personal or family issues going on in my life and stay focused on my models.

I was paid handsomely to lift them toward their dreams, and that's what I tried to do.

I was also competitive; I wanted to outshine other agents. I did not want to become someone ordinary. I wanted to be great at what I did. Every day, I fought hard to bring in every opportunity I could. The only time I settled for less was when God took away jobs that He knew were not right for my models. When that happened, I trusted the words my good friend Melody once said to me: "God did not mean for you to have that booking; it was meant for someone else!"

I thank my God, Jesus Christ, for the eye he gave me in selecting talent who I felt in my heart had the potential to do great things. I thank God for Harold Robbins, who opened my eyes with *The Carpetbaggers* and gave me a dream that would become big and beautiful. I thank my wonderful heroes, Abraham and David, whose lives and words encouraged me to keep pushing forward and keep on trusting the greatest agent ever, God.

God took me from my beautiful, tiny island with only $56 in my pocket, brought me to New York, and turned me into an agent with a six-figure salary. With all my dreams bottled up inside me, He carried me on His wings around the world. He placed me among kings and queens, along palace paths, among ruins, with great fashion models, agents, designers and everyone else, including the hard working messengers who made sure my models' books were delivered on time. Along the way, I always reminded myself that one day I was going to receive great things—until one day I realized I was *already* living an amazing dream! No matter what, God had honored me and brought what I had dreamed of to fruition.

I worked hard to achieve every *Vogue* shoot I'd imagined having, and God was merciful and kind to grant them to me. I don't know why He chose to bless me in such an incredible and beautiful way with a wonderful life and career, but I am grateful that He did.

God is amazing. I've achieved everything, seen everything and gained everything I ever wanted. I am thankful because the Lord walked with me every step of the way as my shepherd and as my agent. For that, I love Him very much. Now I look forward to giving back the love that was given to me by everyone that God blessed to put in my path. Good or bad, they all played a part in making me the person that I am.

When He calls me home, I can leave this world with a smile. This account of my journey to *Vogue* is my way of saying "thank you" to everyone who joined me on my adventures.

God bless!

Acknowledgements

This book was written for my beautiful mom, to whom I owe everything: my faith in, love for and trust in God. I wouldn't be here without her and only wished she was here to 'have a good laugh' while reading it. I miss you Ma, each and everyday, since the Lord chose to take you home, one year ago. This is for you! I love you.

This is also for my beautiful dad, who did not get the opportunity to also see this book to completion. My heart is broken by the loss of you both, but know that one day soon, I will see you both again, in Heaven.

For my brothers Desmond, Frank, Jason, sisters Juleen and Julian, nieces, nephews, aunts, uncles, cousins, in-laws, in London, United States, Canada, Jamaica and everywhere else that each of you are, especially Vivine, Maxine, Stephen, Jacqueline, etc, I love you.

For my beautiful Uncle Roy and Aunt Fay in London, thank you for being kind and gracious to me when you both opened your homes to me.

For Uncle Alan and Auntie, I love you both so much and am thankful for also blessing me with a home back in England…you were more thank priceless, you were the gift the lord used to bless and protect me.

Mrs. Singh, my last landlady in London, thank you for all the curry and the warm milks left at night, after a hard day and night at work. You were more than a landlady to me, and more of a mother; I will never forget your loving kindness.

For a great friend and brother Ken Gray, thank you for always believing that I could be a great agent and for opening so many doors for me; may God eternally bless, guide and protect you all the days of your life and the wonderful photographs that you always take.

Richard Elms, thank you for being such a great friend and brother and for giving me the opportunity to know you and to have you still as close a friend as possible. May God forever bless you and your son.

Melody Washington, the most precious of friends anyone could have in their lives – I love you, sis.

Thanks also to:

Gustavo Pineiro, for being such a beautiful friend; you are loved.

Gara Morse (Elite) for teaching me what to look for in a supermodel.

April Ducksbury formerly at MODELS 1 Agency, London.

Zigi Golding at Z Models, London.

Courtney Bennett and Family, for giving me a place to stay when I first arrived in NY.

Zigi Mueller, an amazing agent and friend.

Linda 'Lily Rose' Morris, for opening amazing doors for me and for being a great friend.

Nike Jonah for being an incredibly beautiful sister and friend. I love you.

Janet Sinclair, the first true model agent I ever knew and learnt the most from; your lessons were priceless.

Brian Levy, for teaching me photography and the art of photograph printing.

Albert Brown, for being a mentor.

Avril Saunders & Cassetta Chin for being my first supermodels

Shaan Ghaznavi for also being one of my first discoveries

Steve Ying and Gary Murphy from Camperdown High.

Adam Gershuny for being a great friend and business partner, even though things did not work out the way we thought it would with the agency. I will always remember your kindness as well as your mom's love to me.

Kingsley Cooper

Valerie Celis, my little princess and 'grandma'.

Lois Samuels, my Jamaican girl

Wendy Brooks

Ben Garcia, my adopted son.

John Moore, for being a friend and brother.

Jorge Estrada, "mi loco hermano".

Christie Dinham.

Pastor Maria at the Unbroken Chain Church and her wonderful congregation

Pastor Cymbala at The Brooklyn Tabernacle and the amazing choir that touches our heart daily and drives us to love the Lord.

Tina, Alex and Ross Steimle for being a great family in Miami and the Dominican Republic

Rev. Garth Thompson, Rev. Earl, Minister Cynthia Lee and Rev. 'Hunter' Thompson at Miami Beach Community Church

Franco LaCosta and his beautiful family

June Joseph

Reinaldo Barnetti and Coco Mitchell

Dominique Veret, my beautiful friend. Je t'aime.

Jimmy Hester, a true and incredible friend.

Paul Fisher & Omar formerly at IT/OMAR Models

Waris 'Grandma' Dirie for opening your heart and story to me; I'm thankful your story of FGM (Female Genital Circumcision) was able to save thousands of young girls lives around the world.

Barbara Walters and Frank Mastropolis of ABC 20/20, for sharing with the world the story of Female Circumcision; your report helped to save many lives.

Michel McQueen at ABC Nightline, for giving me an opportunity to share my voice

George Speros, one of the best agents I've ever had the privilege to work with.

Heinz Holba at NY Models

Jean Luc Brunel; what a blessing to have a friend like you in the industry. Thank you for all the opportunities.

Scott Lipps at ONE Management, for being one of the best agents to work with.

Nikolena Dosen – I love you.

Irene Marie: You are such a beautiful light and one of the most incredible bosses ever to work for. I love you.

Bethann Hardison, you opened the doors for me when no one else wanted to, and for that, I give God thanks and praise for the years I was blessed to work with you, and to learn the art of being a great agent. Thank you! Thank you! Thank you! God bless.

Carolyn Bessette-Kennedy

Arlene Weiss – you are so loved.

Carmela Zigari & Ramulzee: Gone, but not forgotten.

Drew Tal – my Israeli brother: You opened your heart and friendship to me and kept it opened all these years. I love you. Shalom!

Walter Coddington and all the associates at the UN, for helping to spread so much words from FGM to Women's Rights and Children's Rights, especially those with AIDS.

Wendy Fitzwilliam, one of the most beautiful former Miss Universe and a great Ambassador for Children Rights

Kirsten Neuhaus, my agent, for believing in this book

Melanie DeMarco

Michael Waller

Matthew Fox

Tyson Beckford

Jenny Vatheur

Sheila Berger

Silvia Nebauer

Nicole Mitchell-Murphy

For all the models that entrusted me with their career: what were you thinking?

For all the photographers, especially Steven Miesel, Steven Klien, Ruven Afanador, Bruce Weber, etc, and those too many to mention, I'm eternally grateful for helping to make the dreams of my models come true, and by doing so, you changed many lives.

For Trudi at *Vogue* and Preston at *Harpers Bazaar* for continually using our models, and all the other magazines for believing in us and taking so many chances with our young stars.

Thanks to my incredible editor, Tim Vandehey, for rescuing this book.

For all the designers, casting directors, clients, former agents, associates, etc, etc, etc, GOD BLESS YOU ALL…we could not have accomplished all that we achieved without you! Thank you!

And, finally for Abdel…je t'aime!

About the Author

*T*yrón **Barrington** is a former top model agent who's managed the careers of some of the world's leading supermodels and celebrities. In 2003, at the height of his career, he walked away from it all based on his faith and trust in God. Now a top casting director and Producer, he's cast and produced for clients such as Avon Mark Cosmetics, Levi Strauss, Target, L'oreal Feria, Jennifer Lopez, D&G, *Elle*, Cosabella, and NY Kids Fashion Week (Petite Parade), and has produced shoots for celebrities including Lauren Conrad, Ashley Greene (*Twilight*), Lucy Hale (*Pretty Little Liars*), Samantha Barks (*Les Miserables*), R&B sensation Elle Varner, Kat Graham (*Vampire Diaries*), Grace Potter, and Jamie Chung.

Tyron has worked on TV shows such as Bravo's "Double Exposure," the Dutch program "I Can Make You A Supermodel" the Moroccan documentary "Rallye of the Gazelles," and work for BMW International in Jamaica, and has been interviewed on ABC's *Nightline*, and in the *New York Post*, among other media outlets.

For information on Tyron and information on speaking engagements, expert training and consultation on the fashion industry for models and their parents, visit www.TyronBarrington.com.

For every purchase of this book, a portion of the proceeds goes to St. Jude's Children's hospital and Avon Mark cosmetics M.Powerment program, helping to raise awareness of domestic violence and empower women to speak out.

IF YOU LIKED THIS BOOK:

- Tell your friends to go to our Facebook page, click "LIKE" and post a comment
- Tweet "Recommend reading #TheLordIsMyAgent by Tyron Barrington" @LordIsMyAgent
- Tweet your thoughts at #TheLordIsMyAgent
- Instagram at LordIsMyAgent
- Rate it on GoodReads

Made in the USA
Lexington, KY
31 March 2014